"Gerette Buglion's *An Everyday C[ult]* ...
better understand cultic dynamics ...
on the culture at large in this highly personal yet universal story."

—Mark Laxer, author of
Take Me for a Ride: Coming of Age in a Destructive Cult

"Gerette Buglion has quite a story to relate. For over eighteen years,
she was a member of an 'everyday cult,' one that flew under the radar
for almost two decades in the small community where it operated.
Detailing her own treacherous journey from hopeful therapy
client to enthusiastic cult member to anti-cult crusader, Buglion
delivers a clear warning about the destructive power of charismatic,
authoritarian leaders and what it takes to regain one's own inner-
strength and self-awareness. A timely book for both individuals and
institutions."

—Susan Z. Ritz, author of the award-winning mystery
A Dream to Die For

"In *An Everyday Cult* Gerette Buglion shares her passion to educate
others about the prevalence and dangers of undue influence. Few cult
memoirs offer such depth of knowledge about coercive dynamics
and the universal human experience of abuse of power. Her good
storytelling and nuanced writing guide the reader through the twists
and turns of human vulnerability while also inspiring determination,
resilience and hope."

—Steven Hassan, PhD, author of
Combating Cult Mind Control and *The Cult of Trump*

"Gerette Buglion's remarkable book, *An Everyday Cult*, breaks
cultism down to a granular level, shining a light on its everydayness,
especially for those hungry for personal growth, as highly intelligent
and sensitive people naturally are. Through her excellent storytelling,
we learn that when one's reality is constructed by manipulative
forces—no matter how subtle—there is always someone being
enslaved to someone else's will. Breaking this cycle, that is more
prevalent and more subtle than you might think, requires resilience,
vulnerability and creativity. This book shows us that what we

ultimately seek is a democracy of thoughts and emotions and the liberation of the human spirit."

—Artemis Joukowsky, III, director, filmmaker and author of *Defying the Nazis: the Sharps' War*

"*An Everyday Cult* is a raw and compelling narrative. It's told with unflinching clarity, not shying away from the author's faults, emotions, or vulnerability. With everything happening in the world today, Gerette is hoping for a bold new movement that will destigmatize the judgement made about people caught up in cults. This book is a fantastic step toward that goal."

—Joelene Pynnonen, *Independent Book Review*

An Everyday Cult

An Everyday Cult

GERETTE BUGLION

Ingrid,
May my story help lift
the veil, revealing the everyday
cults hiding in plain sight
around us. Thank you ♥
Gerette
#iGotOut

Rootstock 🍃 Publishing

Montpelier, VT

First Printing: 2021

An Everyday Cult Copyright © 2021 Gerette Buglion

Release Date: May 25, 2021
Softcover ISBN: 978-1-57869-055-8
eBook ISBN: 978-1-57869-056-5

LCCN: 2021902973

Published by Rootstock Publishing
an imprint of Multicultural Media, Inc.
27 Main Street, Suite 6
Montpelier, VT 05602 USA

www.rootstockpublishing.com

info@rootstockpublishing.com

For permissions or to schedule an author interview, contact the author at gerette@gerettebuglion.com.

Interior and Cover design by Eddie Vincent ENC Graphic Services (ed.vincent@encirclepub.com)

Cover art by Mary Hill, maryhillstudios.com, photographed by Ward Rice, Stowe Photography

Author Photograph by Lisa Dimondstein

Printed in the USA

for Frederic
without whom, I might still be asleep

and for all of us,
wherever we are in the process of waking up

Foreword

WE ARE OBSESSED WITH CULTS. This is the zeitgeist of our current culture. We want to know how on earth people get sucked in. Why do they stay? What wakes them up? For better or worse, it's the sensational cults that grab the headlines: group suicides, sex scandals, branding, starvation diets, and mass deception. But what about the less obvious groups? The family groups, the organizations, the political groups, or the manipulative partners who gaslight you? What about the everyday cults? How do they work?

Beyond the entertainment and the sensationalism, the abuses aren't proprietary to cults. They thrive in our current society. However, in our obsession with cults, we often dismiss the notion that we can fall prey to such a group, that we aren't susceptible to these abuses. But these things do flourish in our day-to-day lives, and we often don't see them until it's too late.

We wouldn't understand such dynamics if people didn't speak up about their experiences with these groups. Gerette Buglion is one of those brave warriors who courageously share their journey with us.

I met Gerette in the cult-recovery world. One of the silver linings to being public about my personal involvement with a high-profile destructive cult has been meeting so many people involved in cult-abuse education. I never would have met Gerette otherwise. As a whistleblower against Keith Raniere and NXIVM, I have been thrust into a sphere of academics, fellow survivors, and educators. Gerette is one of these new peers who I am honored to know. I was immediately struck by her gentle wisdom and insights as a fellow survivor.

Gerette eloquently describes the shifts in her thinking over the eighteen years in her cult group. Her writing creates a palatable space for the reader to absorb the lingo that overrides and hijacks the mind. Gerette's experience as an educator brings the reader the whole story. She encourages us to peek under the surface and explore the nuances of being human. She invites the reader into a dialogue so that, together, greater understanding can be achieved.

This dialogue is a perfect blend of personal anecdotes and retrospective academic analysis. Her writing is both educational and compelling. I love how she reflects back on moments with her new "awake" eyes. She explains what was happening in reality versus what she *thought* her leader was dictating in his "word salad" doctrine, a therapeutic model that was both transformational and deceptively toxic. As Gerette and I each experienced in our respective communities, cult messaging is a mixture of profound nuggets from legitimate therapy along with poisonous advice that only strengthens the leaders and their agendas.

Gerette brings the reader on her extensive journey of growth and self-discovery amid her quest to be a part of conscious communities and alternative education systems.

Her epic adventure shines a light on what we all want to understand in this current fascination with cults: How do they hook you? Gerette's story, told with unwavering vulnerability, highlights the good that lures people in. As we shared in the documentary *The Vow*, no one joins a cult on purpose. They join what seems to be a good thing. What's the honey on the outer layer of the rotten onion? When you read this book, you will have the answer! And you will know so you don't get lured yourself. What a gift!

You will discover that it's not all Kool-Aid and branding and shaving heads — most cult abuses are more subtle and coercive. Thousands of cults and coercive groups still exist, and this book will show you what to look out for in your own life, for yourself and for loved ones. So you can *see* it. Spot the red flags, whether it be with an exciting workshop, a new therapist, a narcissistic boss, a charming new date off a dating app, or even a political group. Learn to know the difference between toxic ego and legitimate leadership.

Gerette also shares why people stay dependent and are driven to keep going but can never graduate. She explains that "…there is a subtle tension between empowerment and dependence." She highlights what we both now recognize as a telltale sign of cult—it's never-ending. The ranks are endless, the goal posts move. Pro tip: Never join a course, program, or system that you can't graduate from.

For some, this book will also be a glimpse into the juicy bits we all want to know. How are people punished in these groups? What is the intoxicating high of personal growth and why is it so addictive once you start? How does the slow indoctrination work? Why don't the frogs jump out of the boiling water?

Once you have this template, you can see it everywhere. The blinders are lifted and the con is exposed. I believe that many people will relate, especially if you have been part of a cult in the personal growth/therapy world. You will see how our desire to "excavate our psyches" before a group, as witness, can be so thrilling.

Not all cult survivors want to be public, however, and many don't do the personal work needed to figure out *what happened* to them, and how. Gerette, however, not only has a deep passion to expose these abuses, but also to teach the world how cults operate in everyday aspects of society.

I resonated so deeply with this book. Not only am I a fellow cult survivor, but we shared the same passion to *help* people. When each of us realized that we had bet on the wrong horse (as it were), we both pivoted to use the journey to educate others. We share the same motivation to make sure others don't make the same mistakes we did.

This book is a service, but it's also a compelling read. It flows between the author's childhood and different stages of her fascinating time with "the work." Gerette shares her own patterns, the basis for what made her ripe for the leader's abuse. Her book also offers, for those seeking to understand and not judge, a compassionate view of what drives our time with these groups: often simply a desire to belong and to experience life deeply.

Ultimately, to me, this is not a book about a cult. It's a story of a woman reclaiming her voice, bolstered by a passionate desire to hold out a candle of hope for survivors and other victims of injustice. Truthfully, I didn't want it to be over. I want to hear the rest of her life story as she shares her truth. I am glad to know her so I can find out what happens next.

—**Sarah Edmondson,** author of *Scarred: The True Story of How I Escaped NXIVM, the Cult That Bound My Life*

Author's Note

THOSE IN CULT RECOVERY HAVE a decision to make: to identify, or not, the group or leader(s) who have harmed us. For many, naming the organization and those involved is essential for healing. In my current work as a cult awareness consultant, I encourage clients to do so when it empowers them *and* there is little risk of backlash. If naming a perpetrator puts a survivor in danger, I avoid it. In my writing, I do not identify the leader or the group I was involved with. Once I left and immersed myself in the study of cultic dynamics, I gained perspective. The group I previously believed formidable and of great importance to humanity was actually small, and wielded very little power in the world. This new understanding helped orient me. I have additional reasons for not calling out my former teacher, but I will get into those later.

I feel a distinct discomfort in taking up this much space for *me*. A whole book? Am I a narcissist? I remind myself that a lot of us have experienced abuse of power. This book is about me, but perhaps it's about you, too. If there are passages that make you uncomfortable, and I hope there are, please stay with me. I believe, or at least hope, that you will find solace and understanding somewhere in these pages.

Throughout this book, I refer to the group I belonged to as "CTL," short for the Center for Transformational Learning, which, to my knowledge, does not exist. I often reference *"the work,"* a broad term used in many spiritual traditions, encompassing ideology and practices. My teacher I refer to simply as "Doug." Nearly all of Doug's dialogue herein is directly quoted from my recorded sessions and journals. The inspiration for this book is to shed light on cultic dynamics, rather than to expose Doug and his practice.

Identifying details of people and events have been altered to protect privacy. All names and places have been changed—all except for those of my brother Raymond and a childhood family friend named Rip. Raymond, Rip, and John—a beloved friend and former CTL member, are no longer alive. I like to believe all three of their spirits have accompanied me through the writing of this book.

Since leaving CTL, I have been processing *the work*, discerning what was helpful from what hurt. This sorting of wheat from chaff is the hallmark of ethical groups, a necessary culling process to be completed with honest transparency. When we were together, we never did this. As I dig through the rubble, I find kernels of integrity. But there were, probably still are, flaws in the work Doug continues to promote. For some, the flaws are inconsequential, water off a duck's back. For me, they are unconscionable. My previous comrades may believe *the work* was perfect for them, and still is. I understand and respect their perspective. They may believe *the work* started out great but soured over the years. For me, there were problems from day one.

What I have written is mine. Every recollection is real, how I experienced it, and how I wish to express it.

❧

To my CTL brothers and sisters: Your story is yours. Reach out to me, if you want. I welcome creating new relationships from the charred embers of our shared experience. Let's explore neurological gaps, create new synapses, rebuild the turf we gave away, to discover what, if anything, we now have in common in the everyday world.

Introduction

IN MY EARLY THIRTIES, I joined a group I hoped would help me—and it did—but it also gradually eroded my psyche, captured my mind, my money, my time, and my sense of self. I stayed tethered to this group for 18 years, 4 months, and 28 days.

I grew up in a mildly dysfunctional white, lower-middle class family in the Hudson Valley of New York state, moved north at the age of nineteen, and eventually met the man I'm still married to, despite nearly separating from him twice. My husband Frank was involved in CTL for sixteen years, but never bought into it as much as I did. Our daughter, Layla, was six months old when Frank and I each had our first session with Doug, the leader of CTL. Four years later, our son Sammy was born.

I was in a partial and at times complete trance state throughout my children's childhood. This reality is a painful wound; the only salve is their love, forgiveness, and resilience as the young adults they now are. Frank grew weary of Doug's unfulfilled promises and left two years before me. He didn't push me to leave the group, for fear I would leave him instead. And he was right—I *would* have chosen CTL over my marriage. I am humbled and deeply grateful for his insight, patience, and love.

Throughout our years in the group, Frank and I worked various jobs, ran a business, owned our home, and appeared to be autonomous, free-thinking adults. We were not forced to tithe or relocate closer to our teacher. When I snapped out of the group in May of 2014, I reconnected with my pre-cult identity as an educator, and began to study human behavior through the new lens of spiritual abuse and cult dynamics. Having lived through eighteen years of unethical use of power, I now see its tentacles slinking into every layer of society, *if we let them.*

Cultic abuse can infiltrate groups of all kinds—religious, educational, political, commercial, self-help, or cultural—creating what I call "everyday cults." Such groups possess coercive traits that are hidden, whether intentionally or not. Such groups often appear harmless, maybe just a little wacky or obsessed about a particular ideology or leader. Such groups can cause tragic harm if they employ common cultic techniques redesigned to fly under the radar, often appearing perfectly acceptable. Everyday cults are typically small groups where mini unethical power violations occur regularly. However, they are formatted on the same dynamics employed by the likes of Jim Jones, who encouraged 900 followers to take their lives by drinking cyanide laced Kool-Aid in the jungle of Guyana, and Reverend Sun Myung Moon, famous for his mass weddings of thousands of followers. Everyday cults typically move at a slower pace than those whose recruitment systems have been polished. Cumulatively, however, minds, money, and lives are captured for the leader's gain at the members' cost.

❧

This memoir is written in five parts that coincide with the five distinct phases I experienced in my cultic involvement. The first part, "Falling," refers to both falling in love and falling asleep. It is the starry-eyed stage where I was magnetically drawn to *the work*, under Doug's direction, throughout a five-year period that included a lot of longing, learning about myself, and a whole lot of idealizing. Just as no one intentionally falls in love with an abuser, I didn't just *join* a cult—I fell for it.

After "Falling" came an eight-year period of psychological meandering I call "Drifting." Throughout this time, part of my psyche was lulled into unconscious complicity with CTL doctrine while I continued to work as an elementary school educator and a "house mother." In this partial trance state, I was easily influenced but could operate in the world just fine. I lived a split reality, relying on skills I'd developed previously that allowed me to function, but my sense of self was becoming unhinged by my commitment to *the work*.

The third phase, "Asleep," was the most jarring. I could no longer bear my split reality. My psyche had been eroded to the point where the only ground I believed I could trust was *the work*. I became fully dedicated to Doug and the CTL principles, regardless of the impact it was having on my family, myself, and my life. This phase lasted five years, until I snapped out of it.

The fourth phase, "Snapping," was the brief period encompassing the enormous and sudden shift of my conscience awakening—opening my heart and my mind—positioning me back into the center of my own life.

The fifth and ongoing phase of my cultic involvement is my life today, where I have awakened to cultism and remain ever watchful. I call this phase "Waking Up Again and Again."

❧

We live in an age where technology has exponentially expanded the power to influence individuals and groups of people in unprecedented ways. It can be harmless to drift for hours on the web, hopping from lightbulb shopping to energy efficient cars to eventually getting sucked into a friend's divorce drama on Facebook. Worst case scenario, you don't get enough sleep and have to dose up on coffee in the morning.

However, when the rabbit hole is baited by disgruntled ex-intelligence agents and maligned gaming experts, who use images of brutalized children to lure viewers into a new way of thinking, as cult expert Steve Hassan, PhD, describes in his research on QAnon, something else is happening. When deep knowledge of human vulnerability is weaponized, void of human conscience, people get hurt. Minds lose their ability to grasp reality. Friends become enemies. In the anticipation of the next thrilling "Q drop," (the cryptic puzzles 'dropped' into cyberspace that engage QAnon believers) we lose the anchor of our values, the importance of our lives, and don't realize we have actually entered a treacherous rathole (different from a rabbit hole—not just a maze, it is a place of hoarding trash, with more filth and greater danger). To understand how something on this scale happens, we must keep the process in mind. I might be wrong, but I have a hunch that in the years to come, we will learn that QAnon alone may have unduly influenced more Americans than any other cult in modern history.

❧

Vying for power is a biological urge, a survival mechanism at the heart of our species. So, too, is seeking balance, creating reciprocity and opportunities for healing, and, I daresay, expressing and feeling love. Is it possible we are standing at the brink of the greatest opportunity mankind has ever faced, choosing whether to support humanity's evolution or cling to authoritarian systems that prevent this from manifesting?

In my mind, the best antidotes to unjust power are honest dialogue, education, and the cultivation of ethical leadership grounded in respect for Nature's designs, which sustain our existence. To this end, I am honored to be a founding collaborator of a hashtag movement called #iGotOut. What we hope will become a movement like no other, #iGotOut aims to harness the power of honesty and the vulnerability of breaking free from shaming societal voices, by sharing personal stories of abuses of power. Everyone who has suffered from cultic or controlling groups is invited to tell their story. Just as an ecosystem relies on a wide diversity of organisms for longterm sustainability, the #iGotOut movement thrives on stories from every family, culture, religion, or belief system from every layer of society.

Although I do not identify as Christian, I sometimes find solace in my childhood Catholic roots. *In the beginning was the Word, and the Word was with God, and the Word was God.*

The word, once spoken, has the power to open hearts and move mountains.

When our stories are silenced by shame, regret, indifference and fear, this power is thwarted. When our lived experiences of abuse of power are told with honesty, compassion, and love, I believe we will collectively shift closer to a world where unchecked power is dethroned and critical thinking is fostered as a necessary tool, not only for survival but for creating a better world.

I believe humanity's most valuable hidden resource is *conscience*. In my life, conscience was the excruciating moment when I saw that I'd unknowingly supported something in direct conflict with who I truly am. You will learn how my conscience was jolted awake, forcing me to reckon with the ungrounded idolization of my teacher. When individuals recognize that a loved one, neighbor, even a stranger has been hurt by a leader or group that we trust, conscience awakens. Like the leaves of a beech tree on a warm spring day, once awakened, there is no going back to the bud.

❧

I was not alone during my eighteen years in CTL, and I am certainly not alone now. More than anything, I hope my story will give you some assurance that you, too, are not alone.

PART ONE

FALLING

"Falling in love, falling asleep . . . What's the difference?"
– Doug

*"It's like I'm falling in love, devoting myself to the
wonders of the work, the thrilling openings and
surprising twists of discovery. I am a sponge, sopping up
all I can from others,
as I find my way through early motherhood while
opening my mind and heart to a whole new way of
being in the world."*
– Gerette's journal, January 1996

To Flock and to Herd

Mid Winter, circa 1975

"GET UP, YOU LAZY BUM!" Raymond taunts Katherine as he yanks the blankets off her bed. Relieved to be ahead of my big sister for once, I pull on my barn boots and slip into the brisk, pre-dawn quiet just as Kat starts hollering. Dad is gone, away at some methane conference, and my brother suddenly thinks he's in charge. He can be such a prick.

Does it matter that seeds of subservience are being cast into my adolescent psyche, or that grief and mistrust will eventually fracture our Walton-style family—or that I will lose my grasp on reality? Some would say there's no way around it, it's just the way the cookie crumbles. I say indifference is a dangerous mindset. But I am getting ahead of myself.

I head to the sheep shed first. The girls start bleating even before I open the rusty milk can that holds their grain. They nudge me with their black noses and I smile. "Good morning, Molly. Morning, Matilda. Good morning, Anyone." That really is her name. When we picked her up from the Markel's farm, Mom called, "Hey Ray! What do you want to name your sheep? We need to write it on her certificate." Raymond looked at the black-faced wooly wonder he was holding and hollered back, "Oh . . . just call her Anyone!" And, so it was.

I peek out the window from the sheep shed and see Kat trudging toward the barn, scowling. I crack thin ice in the water bucket, see there is still hay in the rack, and tell my small flock, "I'll bring you more hay this afternoon." I scoot outside to catch up with Kat, who glares straight ahead as I fall into step beside her.

"He's such a bastard." I nod in agreement. Kat slides open the door to the milk house and moist warmth welcomes us.

"I'll feed today." I head into the main dairy to the sounds of clanking, metal on metal, as a few of the cows awkwardly rise, stretching their necks through their stanchions. I open the grain chute above the cart and scan the barn as the cart fills.

Chunky is chewing her cud, a good sign that her wound is healing. Sugar, our only Guernsey, looks more like a heifer than a full-grown cow when compared to our Holstein herd. Gracie moos, looking right at me as if to remind me the cart is full.

I snap the chute closed and push into action, measuring grain by full, half, and quarter scoops to each of the ladies—their portion determined by their milk yield. I give Gracie a bit more than her two-and-a-half scoops. Just because. Vache Noir gets one-and-three-quarters; Chunky, two; Sugar, one. I continue down the aisle of thirty. As I turn toward the second row, I hear Kat emerging from the milk house, empty milkers in hand. I pick up my pace, finish feeding grain to the others, and step into the rhythm of wash, strip, milk, finish, dip, repeat. Kat and I finish milking in record time.

Those were the good days—the best years of my childhood and adolescence—before we lost everything.

❧

January 2, 1996

As a new mother, my body is no longer my own. I am filled with raw vulnerability and seek a new orientation to myself. I kiss six-month-old Layla goodbye and slip into the Subaru, feeling a burst of freedom as I cruise through Timberland and head south on Route 101 to Doug's house for the first time. I bring with me a burning question: can this "dream work" help me uncover, once and for all, if I was sexually abused as a child?

For years, I have been haunted by the belief that, in a repressed past, someone violated my little girl body. On this cold December afternoon, I approach Doug's home office and hope my friends are right about him. Sun breaks through the cloud cover; snow crystals sparkle. I take this as a good omen and park beside the stately farmhouse. I check the time, hold my dream journal to my chest, and step out of the car.

I pause. I was sure he'd said to use the front entrance, but the knee-deep snow was broken by only a couple of intrepid people who'd post-holed to the door. Not deterred, I follow suit, snow filling my loosely-tied Sorels. At the door, I hesitate again.

Do I knock? What if he's with another client? I check my watch again: 10:56. Do I stand here in the cold? *No*, I decide, and enter Doug's house, brush snow from my boots, and perch expectantly on a wooden chair just inside the door. A large grandfather clock stands across from where I sit. Tick. Tock. Tick. Tock . . . Tick. It teases me: Who will flinch first?

I think of Pearl and Marie, my close friends and colleagues

from North River Waldorf School, who'd urged me to schedule an appointment with Doug nearly a year ago, when I was pregnant. I'd noticed a change in them after they started doing "*the work*," as they call it. There was a sparkle in their eyes and a gentle smile on their lips when they described what Doug was teaching them about the unconscious, as revealed through their dreams.

A wisp of envy arose in me when I saw the two of them whispering in the school's kitchen. I sensed new intimacy between them when they talked about their dreams and what they called "homework." I wanted what they had. But I knew it was not the right time, so I promised myself to reconsider when my child was a few months old. In the meantime, I focused on childbirth, nursing, diapering, and wobbling through new-mother love that broke my heart to pieces and re-formed me each day.

I startle, even though I'm expecting the clock to dong at the top of the hour. I flinch again when a door on my right opens and a disheveled man with a plaid flannel shirt and unruly hair stumbles toward the door, our eyes briefly meeting. Without a word, he exits. I'm left sitting in a blast of cold air and recognition.

Oh, my gosh—that was John!

I hadn't seen him in nearly five years, since my husband, Frank, led him on a Passage Quest, a weeklong rite-of-passage ceremony. John's ceremony had culminated in a celebratory meal around a campfire at our home. I feel a minor sting that he doesn't recognize me, and muse about how wonderful it is that he is seeing Doug, too. The interior door opens again, and a tall man with a shock of white hair, a five-o'clock shadow, and piercing blue eyes asks, "Ah . . . Ger . . . Gerette? Come on in."

I walk through Doug's office door with the question of repressed sexual abuse burning like a hot ember in my mind. I am terrified, but determined to ask for help. Unable to hold its scorching intensity any longer, I blurt my question early on in the hour-long session. He peers at me from across his wide desk.

"What's your dream?" he asks, and then swivels sideways in his chair and begins pecking with two fingers at his keyboard while I read a description of my dream from my journal.

> *I see Pearl (who used to be a dairy farmer), and she looks washed out, dark circles under her eyes. She introduces me to her new husband, who is also a dairy farmer. I feel uncomfortable as he tells me about the mansion he will soon inherit. I don't trust him, but I see Pearl is listening, eyes wide like a child. A purple silk negligee—a teddy— is hanging on a clothesline, shimmering in the breeze. Somehow, the purple teddy confirms for me that he is abusing her. I worry about their hundred cows and am afraid they are also being abused.*

Doug teaches me about an important difference between emotions and feelings. "Emotions are sticky and want to keep you trapped," he says. "True feelings, on the other hand, are the doorway to the soul and are fluid, like ocean waves, sometimes soothingly calm and other times stormy and unpredictable, but always moving, never stuck."

"Ok," I say, as I write in my journal. I hadn't known what to expect, but am pleasantly surprised to be taking notes. It feels like there is substance to this path. Later in the day, I review my journal and add to my notes:

> Emotions are the product of soul resistance, or "pathology." We all have a true soul self, and we deviate from it for all kinds of reasons. There is a force that wants to keep me away from God, away from my true self.

5

Feelings open you up, and emotions shut you down.
FEELINGS ARE THE GOLD.
 We will mine this gold in my dreams.
 True feelings are the gateway to the divine—and
to my soul.
 The divine works through the soul self.

In our first session, Doug also introduces me to the Jungian term "Animus," the spiritual male who will guide me to my true soul self. According to Doug, the Animus is frequently mistaken for a bad man, because he likes to challenge us. But this is necessary in order to wake us up. In my dream, I believed the sexy teddy hanging on the clothesline was somehow proof of infidelity and abuse, but Doug shows me that my assumptions are wrong. On the contrary, Doug contends that Pearl's new husband is the all-loving Animus, or Christ figure, whom I need to learn to trust.

I'm surprised by his reference to Christ, but it doesn't bother me. As an adolescent, I turned my back on the Bible, Jesus, God—the whole kit and caboodle. I outgrew my Catholic-girl self after my parents divorced. But during my first Passage Quest in my mid-twenties, I made peace with Jesus. I invited Him—the man who walked the Earth—into a ceremony for healing challenging relationships. Later, I discovered "anthroposophy" (it took me a while to pronounce it correctly—an-thro-pos-o-fy), the study of the wisdom of humankind. Its founder, Rudolf Steiner, was an Austrian philosopher who gained notoriety at the end of the nineteenth century for his spirit-based ideals, which became woven into the premise of both Waldorf education and biodynamic farming. As a teacher, I was inspired by a holistic approach to child development, and spent ten years immersed in Steiner's theories based on an esoteric view of Christianity. Frank and I were involved in a fledgling Christian Community Church in the Adirondacks, south of our home, where there was a larger population to draw from. Our daughter, Layla, was baptized in that humble community.

"Pearl's husband is the Animus—the 'Farmer of Farmers.' You can learn a lot from him and count yourself lucky that he has appeared in your first dream," Doug states emphatically. "This is a very good sign. He *wants* to teach you. But, to learn from him you need to be a student, to be humble, learn his language—and, well, become one of the cows in his flock." Doug looks down at my astrological chart on his desk.

I wince at his mistake. *So what if he doesn't know the difference between flocks and herds?* I think to myself. As a kid, I certainly knew the difference. While some of my siblings attended the 4-H Duke County Dairy Club, I opted for the Southern Shepherds. I found my best friend there, who eventually crowned me "Wool Princess" while we cracked-up laughing in front of a roomful of sincere 4-H shepherds, disgracing our families.

My sister Katherine was crowned "Dairy Princess" a couple years before me, so I knew the routine. She got to hang out with dairy club friends on a hay wagon pulled by a brand-spanking-new John Deere at the Memorial Day parade. But I rode in the back of Dad's sky blue El Camino, waving to bystanders with a spinning wheel at my side. For the last quarter mile, a few of my friends leaped into the El Camino, got on all fours, and bleated like sheep whenever we weren't howling with laughter.

I know that cows herd and sheep flock, but on that winter day, as my first session heads to a close, I am not about to quibble over it with Doug.

That was one of a few warning signs I did not heed that day. I don't care that he didn't know a herd from a flock—he was a city boy, after all. But he posed as an analyst and failed to ask me about cows, farming, or abuse—three themes that figured prominently in my dream *and* in my life. Doug applauded Pearl's new husband as the "all wise and loving Animus," while failing to query into my personal experience with farming and abuse.

If he had asked me why I thought the cows were being abused, perhaps I would have described how my father would raise his favorite iron bar and smash it on the backside of Chunky, our spirited Holstein who did not like being bullied into her stanchion. Perhaps I would have told him how I treated Chunky's wounds with iodine and Blu-Kote after my father finally left the barn. I might have even told Doug that I later cried in the haymow. Layer onto this the fact that our farm eventually went bankrupt and my parents divorced within two years, and my core wounds are laid bare. It would be months of sessions, every other week, before Doug even knew I was a farm girl.

Instead of recognizing the dissonance between my goals and Doug's technique, I was intrigued by Doug's lessons about the Animus, whose importance could not be understated. His insights all felt so new, so radically different. In the months and years to come, sometimes the Animus would appear in my dreams as a Christ figure eliciting reverence, or a trusted man who brought me comfort or even turned me on. He could also be goofy, inspiring me to lighten up. But in that very first session, I was taught the Animus is an aggressive trickster, and that I should ignore my instinct not to trust Pearl's husband. Doug would later use the term "The Operative" for this unpredictable character who appeared in my dreams dressed as a thief, a sleazy man who sometimes pointed a gun at my head, or appeared to abuse women and cows.

But now I wonder if Doug's operative idea was a version of the patriarchal authoritarianism I was raised on. "Wait till your father gets home" was my mother's helpless response when Raymond, my red-necked, boundary-pushing brother acted up. My father's belt was never used on us girls, but we all felt the blows.

"He does this to get your attention," Doug claims. "To shake you out of your programmed way of thinking and open your mind to the truth."

I listen carefully, taking notes: True feelings are the doorway to the divine self.

"Of course." I nod in agreement. "I think I get it. So, in the dream, when I felt scared that he was hurting Pearl and the cows, *that* was an emotion. I was jumping to a conclusion, like you said, because there's no evidence in the dream that he was abusing Pearl *or* the cows. So, you're saying, *he's* the Animus. So . . . is *trust* the feeling here?"

"Exactly." He swivels to his keyboard, index fingers excitedly typing. "Homework: Be aware of when you jump to false conclusions. Learn to trust the man. Be part of His flock." While Doug's noisy printer clangs back and forth, he looks at his computer screen and I write a few notes in my journal, reveling in what feels like a new doorway to my soul.

Although I find the distinction between emotions and feelings a bit confusing, Doug promises that my dreams and his guidance will show me the way. As the long hand of the clock inches toward noon, we stand to say goodbye. His parting words stay with me: "Don't worry about whether or not you were sexually abused." He looks me straight in the eyes, the blue of his seem to soften as he continues, "If sexual abuse is an issue for you, it will come up in another dream. I promise."

My mind prickles as he speaks so directly about this taboo. No beating around the bush.

"In the meantime, do your best to put that fear aside. The Animus wants you to be free from wrong assumptions." He sends me off, as the ember of sexual abuse sizzles in the air of his cool confidence.

9

I am elated by his proclamation that my dreams will reveal everything I need, and decide to trust this perspective. *Why not?* I think. I've had so much angst about this for over ten years, but I don't have a single memory of being sexually abused to confirm it. I might as well 'put it aside.'

Could it be that easy—to simply not give it any more attention?

It's a sleight of hand, so easy to miss. It's all about distraction: focus where they can learn something new and exciting, where they are teachable. Let them feel good, special, and minimize what is bothering them. *No need to worry about that now.* Cast the hook, heavy with bait. Let them nibble as long as it takes while telling them what they want to hear. (In cult-recovery jargon, it's called "love-bombing.")

Did he really think that way? Or did he simply believe his own doctrine? I wonder, decades later.

I begin seeing Doug every other week, year-round. For two winters, I tromp through deep snow to Doug's front door for my sessions. One day, when chatting with Marie, she mentions that she uses the back door, which is kept shoveled.

I feel foolish. *How did I not know this?* Because Doug never told me.

Cult expert Dr. Steve Hassan, renowned for his book *Combating Cult Mind Control*[1] and for helping people exit cults since the 1970s, developed the term "control of information." Cult leaders have an uncanny ability to know precisely what information to withhold, when and what to dole out, and to whom. At the time, I believed tromping through snow was an intentional character-building strategy. Everything Doug did and didn't do, said and didn't say, meant something to me.

· ✑

Each year, in late autumn, people came out of the northern woods for the Hostaga—a formal event Doug hosted, where a few of his clients shared their dreams and gave testimony to how their lives had been transformed through his guidance. Gracious Jenny facilitated these events long before she and Doug became a couple. She was gifted in making people feel welcome, providing a heartwarming context for the sometimes-jarring stories that were revealed.

It was a very moving event that brought people in *the work* together, celebrating and honoring the deep soul exploration we were all engaged in. For me, it was like church. Sitting in a room full of well-dressed, sensitive people while listening to presenters describe their inner journey, I felt like a door to my own soul unhinged and said *yes* to an unseen force. I'd witnessed friends—smart, successful people, dedicated to living honestly—light up when they started *the work*, and I wanted to light up, too. Along with many others, I flocked to them, to be with them. We were hungry for the particular medicine Doug offered. We were cowboys, chasing the soul's frontier, eager to wrestle with the unruly and rebellious "pathology" demons we witnessed emerging from our dreams, ready to tackle them in each session with Doug.

We wanted to be more honest, bolder. Doug's renegade approach to dreams was a vehicle for the unflinching scrutiny of our souls. Over the years, we would rise and fall, some drifting away from the flock while others, like myself, stayed close to the shepherd. I opened my heart and strived to identify what Doug called my "resistance to God." In truth, I was shedding my capacity for discernment, blissfully unaware of the hidden wolf before me.

"The fall takes no time and forever," says author Courtney Summers.[2]

Driving home after my first session with Doug, I think to myself, *Pearl and Marie are onto something. This work is powerful.* By sharing my first dream with this man, no longer a stranger, a new world has opened up for me. I am a moth drawn to the flame, hungry for the next dream.

Mother's Blessing

January–March, 1996

I BARELY NOTICE THE SNOWY path to my car. I don't remember driving home, yet soon enough, I'm there, eager to greet Layla who is impatient to return to my breast.

I settle into the rocking chair beside the woodstove and share the insights I've gained from my first session with Doug. Frank listens, his eyes glistening in the fading light. Now that I, too, am initiated, he shares more deeply about his session a week earlier. What he tells me makes more sense now that I have tasted the magic. A flow of energy crackles between us, along with the sound of burning logs. For years, we'd been immersed together in the insight of Rudolph Steiner's anthroposophy, grappling with weighty concepts that inspired us to dig deep, spiritually. But now, a soulful path of dreams entices a new way—a way filled with personal promise, rather than lofty anthroposophical ideals. *The work* is so . . . what's the word? Intimate. And edgy.

Frank and I gaze into each other's eyes as Layla sighs deeply and drifts to sleep. The bounty of life's great mystery is wrapped in a bundle between us and within each of our hearts. New resonance is born. After just one session each, we confirm aloud to each other our sense of great fortune to have started this new therapy.

As Layla wiggles awake, I call to Frank, who has gone to the kitchen to get a cup of tea, "Hey! I almost forgot to tell you. John J. is in *the work*, too! He had a session right before me."

"Cool!" Frank returns, passing me a steaming mug of chamomile.

"Yeah, it was a little funny. I was sitting on that chair by the door, and he came out of Doug's office and bolted. I don't think he even saw me." I smile and look at Frank.

"He's a good man," Frank says, staring into the flames licking at the small round window in our Hearthstone, creosote blackening all but a peephole.

"What was that song he taught us at the end of his Passage Quest?" I ask.

"Oh gosh—he shared so many songs!" Frank searches his memory, grasping for a couple of lines, then begins humming. It comes back to us, John's integration song. Smiling, we sing it to Layla:

"May the long-time sun shine upon you, all love surround you.
And the pure light within you, guide your way home."

We drift into our respective memories, back to John's Passage Quest. I picture the photograph of him standing at our neighbor's pond with untucked flannel shirt and jeans rolled to mid-calf, his bare feet sinking into the soft earth as he bends to the water, hands cupped for a drink. The High Peaks of the Adirondacks and pristine sky as backdrop gave this image a timeless quality. It appeared on the front page of our local newspaper, the *People's Record*, with a caption about Wilderness Passages—the small business we managed for a few years that featured the Passage Quest ceremony.

14

Frank and I grin at each other as Layla reaches for her papa.

❧

I'm eager to share the revelations of my first dream session with Marie and Pearl. Marie is first to hear, as we take a walk on a dirt road near our homes, bundled in matching "sleeping-bag coats." My maroon coat almost touches the snowy ground. Bearing extra postpartum roundness, I look—and feel—like a walrus. Marie is nearly a foot taller than me, and her teal coat barely reaches mid-calf. We're an odd-looking couple, but in the north country practicality rules, especially in winter. We are warm.

Layla is bundled and bouncing in the backpack as we saunter along Travis Hill Road, enjoying wide views of the whitened Adirondack mountains to the north, passing the neighbor's pond where John's picture was taken, years earlier. It's a crisp winter day, sun sparkling on snow, as I share a blow-by-blow description of my first dream session.

"It was intense for me to realize how quick I was to judge Pearl's husband in my dream—for no apparent reason! It's terrible! My mind seems to have a life of its own, making all kinds of conclusions. But . . . do you really think, if I learn to trust the Animus, like Doug says, it will help me?"

"Ah, Gerette." Marie takes a long, slow breath and my mind drifts to the last moment of my session, which was so riveting. To be told I didn't need to worry about whether or not I was sexually abused was powerful. I decide not to bring it up. It feels too personal, too deep to even know how to talk about.

Decades later, the pattern is obvious: Narcissistic leaders can gain popularity and power by addressing taboo subjects with any level of authority. Simple as one, two, three.

Marie giggles, and then gushes in her French-English. "I remember mon first session wiv Doug—it was similair. I tought ze Animus was robbing mon Aunt Milly's house, and I chased 'im away wiv a broom!" We laugh so hard, tears stream down our faces. I haven't had such a good laugh since before Layla was born. When we settle, I ask Marie what her current homework is.

"'Let go of control and feel ze joy.' Dis is de best homework ever!" She wiggles her hips, practically dancing. "*Zee work* is so incredibly helpful," she says. "I see parts of myself zat I was total blind to. I can see 'ow mon control"—she grimaces, clenching her teeth and fists— "eez always interrupting what ze Animus wants for me."

Coming from the somewhat archaic teachings of anthroposophy and Waldorf education, I find the language of *the work* refreshing. Marie's relief is palpable, as she embraces Doug's admonition to let go of control and open up to the joy of self-discovery.

We are quiet, taking in the beauty of the High Peaks in the distance. One of my all-time favorite hikes, Mount Marcy's dazzling whiteness and graceful symmetry draw my heart like a magnet to her rocky summit. Simple formulas imprint themselves into my malleable psyche: Christ equals Animus. Control equals Pathology. Connection with the Animus is the Goal. In my postpartum psyche, simplicity is a sweet joy, like tearing off the ribbon and wrappings from a new toy under the Christmas tree.

"On one level, it is sooo simple." Marie sighs, laughing at Layla, who whips off her hat and flings it to the ground. "Remember zee joy and let go of control! No great mystery here!" I agree, and feel grateful for the newfound sense of belonging to a lighthearted community of the soul.

My friend, Pearl, married into the world of dreams; her husband had been one of Doug's first clients. She knew the terminology of *the work* and related with ease to others who were longtime clients. I met a few of her friends, who'd been seeing Doug for years, at her wedding just months before my first session. These women intimidated me, but I also felt magnetically drawn to them.

Pearl's homespun wedding was six-week-old Layla's first social outing. A few months pregnant, Pearl was radiant, with baby's breath in her hair and a flowing white dress that swirled mid-calf above her bare feet and caressed her growing belly.

&

After she gives birth, I call, excited to tell her I'd started *the work*, and to find a time for our infants to meet.

"Come to my Mother's Blessing!" Pearl exclaims. "Val is hosting it here, at our house."

Mother's Blessings are gentle affairs; a ritual developed, by moms connected to North River Waldorf School, as an alternative to a baby shower. The new mom is pampered with a foot soak in warm, rose-scented water, where flower petals float in a wide ceremonial bowl. She sits on a throne, draped with colorful cloths, a crown of flowers adorning her head. We sing softly to her:

> "How could anyone ever tell you
> you are anything less than beautiful?
> How could anyone ever tell you
> you are less than whole?"

Thus, we weave a tight feminine cocoon of warmth, support, and unconditional love. We take turns sharing words of wisdom through poems we've brought as offerings, or heartfelt sharings of our own trials and tribulations. We laugh and often cry, then sing some more.

17

❧

I sit beside my mother in a little white church. I am a teenager but feel like a little girl. I love listening to my mother singing hymns. Soaring soprano notes rise beyond the arched ceiling, straight to the heaven I still believe in. I don't sing, but she does. By proximity to her, I feel closer to God. I walk down the aisle, stick out my tongue, and tilt my head back to receive communion.

❧

By the time I actually start *the work,* my desire for it has been simmering for years, a hunger not immediately fulfilled. A cauldron of longing inside me fueled a fire, fanned the flames of want, of need. While I wait for my moment to begin dream sessions with Doug, and through my first months in *the work,* I desperately long for the ingredient Pearl and her friends seem to possess, which I lack. I want to belong.

Based on the spontaneity of Pearl's invitation, I surmise my presence at her Mother's Blessing is an afterthought, but I'm still delighted to go. I want to connect with Pearl, and be around her friends who'd been doing *the work* for years. Now, I have a few months' worth of sessions under my belt and am excited and nervous to share the experience, be in their presence, and try to fit in.

Pearl's Mother's Blessing lacks the familiar structure I had grown to trust. From the sidelines, I watch the women facilitating, and feel like a fish out of water. Between them is a synergy that is foreign to me. They are cavalier in sharing sex stories, which shocks me—references to penises and vaginas and a level of gaiety that feels incongruous, but intriguing. One buxom woman talks about the "great penis in the sky," and they all laugh. Except me. I don't get it.

Pearl seems comfortable in her body in a way that I'm not. She tosses around terms like "Archetypal Support" and "Pathological Guilt" with ease, and talks about the Animus as "The Operative," as if she knows him personally. She banters back and forth with her friends in this foreign language.

Later, I bring my confusion and feelings of unworthiness to Doug. I also share a snippet of a dream I had shortly after the Mother's Blessing:

Pearl and Val are laughing together.

Doug helps me see how, in this dream, I'm separate from them. They are intimate, but I'm not. We explore my insecurity, which he says is rooted in pathology. During this session, he tells me about Pearl— that she's had her own struggles with insecurity over the years but has grown spiritually in her second marriage. He also tells me that Val was abused in her childhood and couldn't bear to make eye contact with anyone until she started doing *the work*. Doug speaks openly about others, and I assume this level of transparency is part of *the work*. It makes me hopeful that I, too, could someday have the kind of intimacy those women share. My homework from this session is to feel the pain of separation and my desire to connect.

"You have to get to the root, and surrender. True feelings will resonate, because they are expressions of the soul. Feel the pain and see what dreams come to you next."

My intrigue was strong. I vowed to myself to learn as quickly as I could. I challenged my nerdy assumptions and let my hair down, bit by bit. I felt blessed by this new infusion of energy in my life. If my friends and my husband benefited from *the work*, then so could I. Finally, I was drinking from the chalice, tasting the elixir that promised to set my soul free.

❧

After I snapped out of CTL, Marina and I sat in her kitchen sipping tea. I must have told her something I'd learned about another person in one of my sessions.

"Oh . . . My . . .God!" Marina started slowly, strongly, her quiet voice growing with emotion and intensity. "What ever happened to clear boundaries in the therapeutic relationship?!?" Her eyes were wide with horror.

I was jolted, once again, into my growing awareness of the violations I'd been blind to while I was in *the work*. For over a decade, Marina watched me become more and more entrenched, until we drifted apart. Post-CTL, Marina became one of my best friends and greatest allies, providing a sounding board that rose out of her lifetime study of human development and her profession as a nurse practitioner.

For eighteen years, I'd believed I was in a flawless form of therapy imbued with integrity and the potential to truly transform lives. Today, I know unequivocally—*no* path that promises human redemption is perfect, and acknowledgment of this imperfection can motivate adherents into honest, transparent reassessment of the leadership and power structures involved. Without ethical, professional boundaries and a process for ongoing and engaged reconciliation and discernment, such organizations will inexorably slide toward abuse.

Pathology

EVERY GROUP HAS ITS LINGO, especially controlling groups. I was an educated thirty-three-year-old when I started *the work*, but I'd had no previous association with the word "pathology."

But my best friend Sylvie did.

As a physician, she knew pathology as the science of disease. My obsession with discovering and hunting down "my pathology" was not only confusing, it was downright concerning to her. When I stopped working with Doug after eighteen years, Sylvie confided that she'd sought therapy to deal with her own pain and confusion about me and *the work*.

"Every time I heard you say 'my pathology,' I wanted to scream," she said. "It was like nails on a blackboard."

❧

January-February, 2000

Cars are packed into Doug's driveway like sardines. Frank and I pull

21

a little past the house and straddle our vehicle between the lawn and the shoulder of the road. More cars pull up as Frank offers me a hand getting out of the car. Six months pregnant and feeling full-term, I'm grateful for the help. We tromp across the snow to the basement door of Doug's farmhouse.

Attending the monthly "Burn" class has been providing us with the broader arc of *the work*, which has three distinct phases that serve as nodal points in one's progress. These phases are not fixed in stone—they can overlap or circle around rather than proceed neatly, one after the other, but they provide a sense of direction for the seekers gathered in Doug's basement classroom.

"Phase One work is all about uncovering and discovering pathology," Doug says with a sigh, as if he's gone over this a million times. By this time, I know that "pathology hunting" is key to making *the work* revolutionary; we don't shy away from seeing the hard stuff. Since there are new students in the Burn class, Doug is doing some review.

"Pathology lives in every one of us," he states. "It has a will of its own that wants to shut the client down and cut off all possibility of experiencing the true self. A classic Phase One dream shows the client how they get all twisted up in trying to control their spouse or kids."

Frank and I exchange knowing eye contact. We've been through many rounds of trying to control each other, and had a major breakthrough when I let go of my desire to pursue my work as an education consultant. Frank really wanted a second child. Doug's guidance helped me to release control, and Frank and I opened ourselves to greater vulnerability and intimacy with each other.

I shift in my seat and cup my hands over my growing belly. The growth of our family reflects our love for each other and for *the work*.

Doug continues. "Pathology's *job* is to keep the client confused, stirring up emotional reactivity, keeping him unaware of his true feelings. He's utterly lost—from himself and from God. But he doesn't know it. That's the hard part."

As Doug strides over to the bountiful food table, students swivel in their seats, watching him. He pops open a cold Lemon Pellegrino, takes a long swig, and goes on, gesturing with his free hand for emphasis. "Every client—no matter what their particular issues are—has to learn that pathology is in the driver's seat of their lives most of the time. In Phase One work, you've got to reckon with this reality and stare down the inner force that is a master manipulator. But"—he takes another sip, sets down the can, and heads back to the front of the room—"pathology is in fact"—he faces the class, some of us scribbling notes, others listening intently—"a *separate entity*." After a pause, he continues. "It's not the true self. This is really important. Pathology is *not* the person—it's what makes you *less than* the person you are meant to be.

"We can't get to the true self—except for glimmers here and there—until the pathological behaviors have been exposed. But, as most of you in this room already know, this is easier said than done. Why?" Doug often teaches through asking questions—the sign of a good teacher, I note.

Someone calls out from the back of the room. "Because no one wants to see their shit!"

Doug nods, but he's clearly looking for more. He scans the silent room. John's hand slowly raises and Doug steps toward him. John's voice is tentative, but filled with emotion. "Because pathology knows how to hide." Doug asks John to repeat what he said.

"Because pathology knows how to hide." His voice is steady, but from across the room I see John's left hand twitch in his lap.

The room is quiet as we take note of pathology's sneaky trait. Doug paces the front of the room. "There's still more."

Pearl looks up at Doug from the front row. She is one of the wise ones. He nods, encouraging her to speak. She talks so quietly, Doug asks her to say it again, louder.

"Because we over-identify with our pathology," Pearl shouts. "Because we like it!"

"Because we like our pathology," Doug repeats. "We *like* our pathology."

The room has gone silent. It is a weighty moment. Doug looks around and says with a wink, "This is a good time for a break."

I sit with my notebook, musing and digesting Doug's teaching while others chat and eat. Four years into *the work*, I am hearing Doug's description of pathology in a new way, and I consider how I've over-identified with mine. I write in my journal:

> Pathology is not who I am—it's an outside force that
> wants to prevent me from being who I am. How do I
> *like* my pathology?

~

> *I dream of nighttime. I am lying on the ground, feeling*
> *confused and anxious, near a barn. Light is streaming out*
> *of the open door of the barn. I want to go in, but I feel*
> *paralyzed.*

Doug asks, "Have you felt this before—this anxious confusion, being outside the barn, in the dark—is this familiar to you?"

"Yes." Squeaks out of me, defying the enormous wave of feeling that accompanies it. I have felt like an outsider much of my life. In my own family. In my work. Even in my women's group. No matter what I do, I have an underlying sense that I don't belong, that I am imposing on others just by my existence. It is a raw, excruciating feeling, but Doug is excited about it. He tells me this dream is progress, because there are no other players—no one else to blame for keeping me outside the barn. Just me and my pathology.

What *is it* really, that keeps me frozen outside the barn instead of entering it, my place of solace? Doug teaches me about pathological shame, fear, and unworthiness through this dream. My homework is to recognize when, in my day-to-day life, I feel confused and anxious—outside the barn. When I notice this—and I do, often—I am to take a breath, imagine the light radiating from the open door, and know that He, the Animus, the divine father, is in the barn waiting for me. I can go to him.

"It's ok to feel fear." Doug clarifies. "Just don't let the shame and unworthiness keep you from being with Him in the barn."

I love this homework. I notice I feel anxious when I call a friend to schedule a playdate for Layla, and when I talk to a colleague about the school budget. I take a breath and imagine the barn in the night with an open door, light spilling out, creating a welcome mat for me. When I remember to do this, my inner landscape changes—just like Doug promised. Anxiety and confusion melt into vulnerable fear, "the good kind of fear," says Doug. The negative voices in my head that make me an outsider are quieted.

I am blinded by the light radiating from the barn, by the power of the Father's love, steadfast and enduring, so much greater than my quibbling worries about whether or not I am worthy enough for my daughter's friends.

I experience the generosity of God's love for me, for the child who grows within me, and for Frank and Layla, too. Our sweet family is precious beyond words, beyond my capacity to articulate. I start to recognize the many ways I behave like a stranger, or worse, an intruder. I keep taking deep breaths, as Doug encouraged me to, and a miracle unfolds: I soften.

I feel scared and vulnerable, and imagine myself standing with the night at my back, facing the warmth and bountiful light inside the barn. And I enter the barn. That edgy, anxious feeling of being on the ground outside the barn melts like butter in the sun. I can almost feel my pulse settle. I know I am exactly where I need to be. I place my hands on my belly and feel a distinct kick. Life is good.

Just like getting out of a bad marriage, when we leave a controlling group or cult, there is a tendency to throw the baby out with the bathwater. Despite tragic and sometimes irreconcilable harm, these groups and their leaders almost always offer their members something truly helpful. This teaching from Doug is an example of how I was helped, how I gained insight around an insecurity. And when that was identified and reckoned with, my inner development was truly supported.

❧

As one enters Phase Two work, significant changes occur. Since the terrain of pathology is now known, a door opens to relationship with the divine realms. The Animus and the Anima, the Child Self and Archetypal Animals, all become living beings rather than abstract concepts. However, in order to experience *true* relationship, Doug teaches that an alchemical process must occur.

"The primary ingredient of Phase Two is what?" Doug asks in the Burn session.

Several students call out, "Relationship with the archetypes!"

"I didn't realize so many of you were listening!" He smiles. "We could say the archetypes exist to make us more human, more fully who we are destined to be. We can't become our true self without help from the archetypal realm. But there's one barrier—one niggly, little hinderance that keeps most of us from establishing an authentic relationship with archetypal beings. Which is . . .?" He scans the class. His gaze settles on Jenny, one of his best students.

She somberly says, "We have to die first."

&

I am outside, at a park with friends and kids. The sun is setting. A man walks past us, and I am suddenly terrified, paralyzed. He turns around and points a gun right at my head. I scream.

"This is it, Gerette! The moment we've been waiting for!"

I knew Doug would be excited when I brought this dream to him, but I still can't shake the terror. I understand the *theory* about dying to self—that in order to open to a life infused with divine inspiration, my ego, which is attached to my pathology, needs to go—but it is a whole different thing to be shot.

"You have to do this homework like your life depends on it!"

We look at each other and laugh. "You mean, my death depends on it!" I say. It feels good to laugh. Sometimes I get too damn serious. I am aware of what Doug calls my "pensive pathology," where I overthink everything.

"Lighten up and let the man shoot me" is my homework.

Robert Jay Lifton is a giant in the cult recovery world, but only by accident. As a psychiatrist in the 1950s, Lifton worked with Korean prisoners of war and researched the tactics of control used in

Communist China. He published work on what he called "the eight deadly sins of ideological totalism," and was discovered by people who'd fallen into—and gotten out of—notorious cults, including the "Moonies" of the Unification Church, and the red and purple-clad followers of Rajneesh.

The "eight deadly sins" provided those in cult recovery with an understanding of their cultic experience. A link between political extremism and cults was established through Lifton's seminal work on thought reform—more popularly known as brainwashing. Lifton identifies one of these sins as "Doctrine Over Person," in which a doctrine, complete with its mythical elements, is assumed to be "more valid, true, and real than any aspect of actual human character or human experience."

In any group that is identified by an overarching doctrine, the leadership faces an ultimate choice: to validate and encourage autonomy, *or* to enforce control through subtle or overt means, by imposing the group's creed and assuring that, one way or another, members fall into line.

As Doug teaches it, the ultimate goal of *the work*, aside from the ongoing discovery of self, occurs in Phase Three. This is when one's lifework is infused with, guided by, and becomes synonymous with God's plan.

More than four years into *the work*, I still relate to Phase One challenges, but I know my inner work is deepening beyond this. I diagnose myself to be wavering somewhere between Phase One and Phase Two, but after I feel a "breakthrough" of understanding surrounding my dream with the gunman, I sense that I am glimpsing Phase Three.

Doug remains silent when I ask if I am entering Phase Three work. So I become silent about it, too.

My unconscious decision not to challenge Doug about my progress in *the work*, after nearly five years of it, stems from the complex and subtle power dynamic at play. No one graduates from an everyday cult, because the leader and organization around them depend on continued loyalty. Dependence is woven, consciously or not, into policies and decisions. In an everyday cult, there is subtle tension between empowerment and dependence. With no overt system of control, opportunity for authentic progress is essential to keeping people engaged, though never enough to set them free.

A multi-threaded line with many fine hooks is cast into the group's still waters. Nourishing tidbits are plentiful, and the hooks are so small one hardly notices them. For some, the line has plenty of slack, others are held more tightly. Some slip away before the hook sets, and the group sighs, "It's their loss. I hope they come back." The group leader has the uncanny ability to know exactly how much tension or freedom to give each individual who responds to the bait: just enough to entice them to nibble a while longer while the hook settles in deep—and we believe that a little pain is part of the path to freedom.

Spiders

FRANK AND I LOVED BEING involved in *the work*. It ignited a new flame in our marriage reminiscent of when we'd met, ten years earlier. I'd been living at Wyvern, an eclectic alternative community in New York's Monarch Region. Nestled in the mountains, with crystal clear waters surrounding us, Wyvern, named for the winged, two-footed dragon whose tail sports a diamond-shaped tip, was a cool place to live.

The founders were dilettantes, inspired by the wyvern mythology and by diamonds. They constructed an extraordinary multi-family residence centered around a five-story, diamond-shaped community building. For two years, I lived in the highest bedroom and scaled three ladders every night to get there. My roommates had two ladders and one ladder to climb, respectively. Our shared bathroom had no walls. It included wooden sinks and an open-air bathtub set on a loft above the kitchen, twenty feet below. When taking a bath, I could chat with my roommate in the kitchen and watch spiders in the ceiling weave a magnificent web.

Frank and I were introduced through a mutual friend, a Passage Quest guide. We all sweated buckets and prayed for insight during ceremonies in a portable sauna we hauled out to the pond. We called on our ancestors for support, and were dedicated to the rites of passage. We sat naked beside sparkling rivers, notebooks in hand, writing a business plan for Wilderness Passages. We backpacked, and canoed, and hiked, and went winter camping; Mother Earth was our playground *and* our home.

When I became lead kindergarten teacher at North River Waldorf School, our lives turned domestic, more predictable, and our spiritual focus turned to anthroposophy, the philosophy behind Waldorf education and biodynamic gardening. From our mid-twenties to mid-thirties, Frank and I traveled the esoteric depths of Rudolph Steiner's ideologies, both of us completing intensive anthroposophical training.

Decades later, when I attended my first ICSA (International Cultic Studies Association) conference as an ex-member of a cult, I met people who'd experienced cultic abuse through their involvement with anthroposophy and Waldorf education. That was an eye-opener. After a period of feeling defensive, I began to see that the esoteric path I'd been devoted to also dished out a polarized mindset (i.e., black crayons and plastic toys are evil), and had compelled me to work long hours for pitiful pay. Although I did not experience abuse in my work as a Waldorf teacher, the undeniable fact that others did helps me see the threads of authoritarian-style thinking therein. I believe that experience and training predisposed me for my attraction to Doug and the Center for Transformational Learning.

After a decade of teaching, studying, working hard and, more recently, raising children, our lives felt perhaps *too* predictable, too stuffy. Frank and I believed *the work* would make us better parents for Layla (and later, Sammy) and would support our professional pursuits. By focusing on our dreams, we dove deeply into personal waters infused with Christ-consciousness, dedicated to personal freedom and unflinching scrutiny of our shadow side.

I recorded Doug's words in my journal:

> Every dream comes from the Archetypes and is infused with the ability to show the dreamer precisely what is holding him back from his true soul self. In this way, dreams tell us in no uncertain terms where our pathology is hiding. And what we need to do to expose it, so we can get on with our lives as men and women of God.

Sheltered in the embrace of the Adirondack Mountains, Doug developed a novel approach to dream exploration. His work felt compelling and life changing, and we were hooked. Biweekly individual therapy sessions quickly became a focal point for our inner life, as well as a financial priority in our household. Before long, we added couples sessions to that tonic. Money was tight, but we lived simply, sharing our house with roommates, eating from our bountiful garden, and taking on extra jobs to make ends meet.

❧

I share each new homework assignment with Marie or Pearl. We talk for hours, to discover the places where insight from our dreams and the homework Doug prescribes shed light into our lives, and how it supports our decision making, parenting, and our relationships. Although I maintain other friendships, especially in my women's group, I am unaware of my gradual turning away from those who are not doing *the work*.

Showing up at Doug's office every other week is titillating—I never know what gem he will pull out of my dreams. His cut-to-the-chase approach is refreshing, after years of sitting with the often stoic "anthropops" in endless study groups at North River Waldorf School. Doug is a cowboy, committed to speaking the dream's truth, no matter what.

❧

Frank and I continue to attend the Burn, where brave individuals volunteer a few of their dreams to be openly explored, alongside their astrological birth chart, in a no-holds-barred public session.

It's John J.'s turn, and Doug is teaching about the inner child who appeared in John's dream as an abandoned, misshapen waif in a dark alley. "With the child self, we are dealing with something that goes past fear and all the other issues, into something much deeper," Doug says. "It is the essence of how God sees you." He looks directly at John, with a smile. "And in your case, your inner child is a misshapen waif."

A cloud passes quickly across John's eyes. Someone asks, "So, Doug, if that's the case, how do you heal the abandoned child?"

"Don't ask me, I'm just a clerk!" Doug often scoffs at himself. Smiles and quiet chuckles ripple through the class. He makes self-deprecating comments when he teaches, referring to his many years as an uneducated civil servant. Then he gets more serious.

He looks directly at John, his tone softening. "I don't do the healing. The Animus does. God does. That is the miracle of it. God exists. If we are willing to be laid open, to look honestly at our dark side, He can take *anything* and transform it. The archetypes do this for God. They do it for us.

"I work for the Animus. I do whatever He asks. He is God's son, and I trust Him more than I would begin to trust a p-p-person." Every so often, a stutter grabs a word, giving us all a few seconds to take in

Doug's humanness. He rubs his chin and looks up, beyond the ceiling.

"You have to learn the language of the dreams. It is different—often the opposite of what we are used to. The archetypes are coming from God's view, unlike us shallow humans." He adds, "That's why I work for Him. I had a dream early on where He asked me to be His foreman. I said 'yes.' I've been His right-hand man since then."

Feeling tightness in my throat, I close my eyes. For a moment I don't know where the floor is. I say a silent prayer, asking God to help me to see myself with honest eyes.

But I don't ask for help to see Doug with honest eyes. A pedestal is being built for him in my mind, constructed from what I believe is rarefied spiritual integrity.

Doug's belief in himself—in his direct downloads from God—is an assertion that begs for a pulpit to preach from. Authoritarianism depends on this kind of audacity, hierarchy, and followers. My psyche unconsciously responded to an unfortunate magnetic pull that seeks to dumb-down people by curtailing critical and creative thinking. The magnet is made from a compelling ideology, the promise of purity, of transcendence. Instead of being lifted into personal agency, we revere the doctrine.

❧

Early on, Frank and I discover the power of a couples session to reduce marital tension. These sessions are nothing short of revolutionary for us.

We settle on the soft, L-shaped couch in the sitting room adjoining Doug's office. With no big desk between us, Doug relaxes into his armchair, coffee mug in hand, and casually asks, "What's up?" I bite my lip and nod to Frank. In the car on the way over, he said he wanted to start. I figured we'd be talking about car maintenance.

"Well, it's been a pretty good month, except Gerette keeps nagging me about car stuff," he says. Doug already knows what's up, from our personal sessions. He knows precisely how our pathologies manifest and go after each other. I'd been complaining about our car, because I'd dreamt I made a mess of trying to change the oil. Doug also knew about the battle I'd been fighting to get a new couch, and how I'd gotten caught up in a drama at the Waldorf school. He knew Frank was being a tightwad, and espousing a concept that was not grounded in his homework or in our couples homework.

In these sessions, one of us was typically "in the hot seat"—our pathology having a heyday, preventing both of us from moving forward in our spiritual work. Today it was my turn.

"Can't you just let him take care of the cars?" Doug asks. "You are a control freak, Gerette. This control pathology of yours knows exactly how to trigger his insecurity, which leads to anger and resentment." I start weeping, seeing how my pathology is attacking the man I love most.

Doug keeps going. "You guys keep going after each other. You need to stay on opposite sides of the boxing ring. Domains! You each need to stay in your domain. You get to do the laundry however you want to. And Frank gets to decide how to maintain the cars. Can you agree to this?"

Frank's eyes brim, too. With Doug's guidance, our respective pathology is outed and put back in its place. We make agreements and vow to hold each other accountable, in love. Doug's capacity for remembering what we'd discussed in our individual sessions astounds me. In the course of one hour, we feel our marital mess flayed, hashed, and then sutured with new perception. A sense of catharsis washes away the dirt. It feels like spring, no matter the season.

❧

Five years into *the work*, Sammy is born, completing our family constellation. After a short maternity leave, I dream these dreams and bring them to Doug:

> *I'm at a river. I have a kayak, and I'm excited—but nervous, too. I was hoping for flat water, because it's been a long time since I paddled rapids—but these are big rapids. My brother Raymond meets me. He carries an open boat down to the river. I don't know if I can paddle these rapids, but am glad to be with my brother.*

and

> *Huge spiders with enormous egg sacks hang from the ceiling of our kitchen. I'm alarmed at the thought of spiders hatching in the house, and ask Frank to get a bucket. I see a mother spider with a huge egg sack and whack at it lamely, trying to kill it, but don't. I feel bad about trying to kill a spider.*

and

> *I am with a man in a room filled with spiders. There are hundreds of them dangling from the ceiling. I watch as the man takes a big one, holds it between his thumb and forefinger, and inspects it carefully. Then he squishes it with his fingers. I am horrified.*

By now, I know that each session with Doug is both a battle and a blessing. The battle relates to how dense I am to his identification of the dream's teaching, how resistant I am to following through with my homework, and how I get caught up in my pathology. The blessing: feeling the resonance, sometimes not until the very end of the session, when the messy threads are tied together by Doug's insights, and I receive my new homework assignment.

In this session, the battle takes place through the spider dreams.

"The spiders are your damn pathology, Gerette!" Doug pounds a fist on his desk for emphasis. "Can't you see that?!? They want to take over your house and run your life. Destroy your marriage! Screw up your children! *You* have to be the one to kill the spider. The Animus is showing you how to do it."

I lamely protest. "But spiders are . . . special." Gazing out Doug's window, my mind flits back to my days living at Wyvern, where my roommates and I lived in harmony with the spiders in the cathedral ceilings. When one occasionally descended her web toward the kitchen table, we would shoo her back up, saying, "You get the high spaces; we get the kitchen." And she would oblige.

Now my dreams are telling me I need to *kill* spiders?!? Doug has been teaching me for a few years that my pathology is "icky" and overly sympathetic. Now, I reckon I've been caught. Doug helps me see how much I want to protect my "precious pathology" and be altruistic when I carefully remove spiders and gently place them outside, where they belong.

"Altruism is just another version of arrogance," Doug says. "Go ahead and put them outside. The second you turn your back on them, those pathology spiders will creep back in!"

The blessing of this session comes from the first dream: being at the river with my big brother, my one and only brother, Raymond. Doug invites me to close my eyes and picture being beside my bro, imagine getting into his open boat and running the rapids with him.

I am not running the rapids alone. It's scary but thrilling. This is the kind of fear that can carry me to greater intimacy with the Animus.

"It's not about your brother—it's about what he represents in your psyche. He is waking up your inner courage, your desire to ride the spiritual rapids."

When I was in my twenties, Raymond and I pinky-promised to do some big adventure together, like climb Kilimanjaro or paddle the Colorado River. We were still kids then, and believed there'd be plenty of time. He'd left home as a young man, chasing the good money to be made in the oil industry. He labored first as a roustabout, working up the ranks to become a driller. Hard, hard labor. He was solid muscle. A real cowboy—hat, rattlesnake boots, and a rodeo-scene belt buckle engraved with his nickname, "Rat." Raymond roamed the globe for oil jobs, from Louisiana to the North Sea.

"Cold as a witch's tit in January," he'd complain about his stint in Scotland. "From there, I had to thaw out, so I went to Saudi Arabia. Ahh . . . Bring on the heat. 105 degrees—120! The hotter the better. Good, dry heat!" He finally settled in Phoenix, Arizona, far from his six sisters and our divorced parents. All of us girls had found homes and husbands in the Northeast. Ray and I didn't see much of each other, but we talked often about adventures.

That was before he left this world in a dark mess. I didn't know, couldn't know, there would be so little time. I had my family and I had *the work*, and it didn't cross my mind that Raymond's appearance in my dream, with his open boat, may have been a wake-up call to connect, to do more than just talk. Doug didn't see it that way, so I didn't either. I was content to imagine running the rapids with my brother, not knowing how much I would ache for him later.

"Yeah, I'll ride the rapids with Raymond. No problem," I assure

Doug. But I don't say anything about the spiders.

He looks at me from across his oak desk and says, "Feeling the fear breaks the guilt of killing the spiders." I look down at my journal, pretending to write something. He goes on: "Fear is the archetypal feeling. Guilt is just a distraction."

He taps away with two fingers on his keyboard, then hands me a printed copy of my homework. It reads, "Kill the fucking spider! And go into the Rapids with Ray."

Walking to my car, I pause to greet John J., who is arriving for his session. We seem to have landed on the same schedule every other week.

"Good session?" he asks.

"I'm not sure yet." I shake my head. He stops and looks at me with compassion.

"Yeah. Sometimes this work is intense. But it's worth it. Hang in there." He squeezes my hand as he heads in to Doug. I appreciate his words of encouragement. I'm used to feeling elated, or at least thoughtful after a session, not . . . whatever it is I'm feeling right now.

I take a deep breath, determined to start killing spiders— metaphorically—to free my soul, and physically, to prove I am no longer a sappy, overly sympathetic wuss. Through the homework, consciously imagining squishing spiders and riding rapids with Raymond, I hope the battle will settle, as Doug promises, and the blessings grow. As I turn the ignition, I ignore my shaking hand and drive home.

In some circles, spiders are sacred. In some cultures, *all* beings are revered. To me, spiders and their intricate weavings possess a feminine gesture of creativity. They deserve certain respect—like the respect my Wyvern roommates and I playfully, though sincerely, gave them. It would not have occurred to us to kill the spiders. After this session, I became a spider killer. I forced myself to step on them. I toughened up and became less sympathetic, believing I was "busting my pathology" and opening up to support from the divine realm. This, I was taught, was the shift from early Phase One work into the beginning of Phase Two, as *the work* deepened for me. I believed what I was taught: this was progress.

Now, I look back and feel compassion for myself. I see how doggedly I was trying to fit the roundness of my soul into Doug's jagged framework. I see how I suppressed core parts of myself. Recalling the jarring moment in the dream when the man squishes the spider still sends a jolt through me. Was this dream designed to wake me up, to snap me out of the navel-gazing that Doug prescribed, to show me that I was involved in a destructive process? If I insert Doug as the man squishing the spider, this dream carries new meaning.

❧

From the beginning of time, the area I call home has been the homeland and traditional hunting territory for the Kanien'kehá:ka (Mohawk) people. I've learned they are a society that reveres women as the holders of hereditary lines, and live in a harmonious, sustainable relationship to the Earth and all her inhabitants.

Their birthright of integrated, respectful lifestyle with the Earth has long since been buried by my colonizing ancestors. Misogyny has been deeply embedded in American culture for generations now. It never occurred to me that a man in my dream, studying and then squishing a spider, could be nefarious. Over the course of five years, I'd adopted a new form of communication, imbued with spiritual overtones that hid its controlling nature. I'd adopted this language, recognizing how it offered me another way of relating to others—and myself. But I didn't realize I was suppressing my core values in the process. Since leaving *the work*, I have returned to my gentle relationship with the natural world and her creatures.

Post-CTL, I helped clean my neighbor Elizabeth's home for extra cash. On my first day, she lilted in her soft British accent, "Oh, and by the way, if you find a spider, please don't kill it. Either leave it be or bring it outside." When she left for her walk, I allowed tears to flow and smiled as I carried a few spiders outdoors on my feather duster.

I do this and reclaim pieces of my soul. Essential as the air I breathe.

PART TWO

DRIFTING

"There is a brief time, between waking and sleep, when reality begins to warp. Rigid conscious thought starts to dissolve into the gently lapping waves of early stage dreaming, and the world becomes a little more hallucinatory, thoughts a little more untethered."

–Vaughan Bell, *The Atlantic*, April 2016 [3]

Leaving Home

July 1, 2003

TORRENTIAL RAIN PELTS THE WINDSHIELD and creates rivulets down our driveway, obscuring my last view of home. Layla is just big enough to peek over the dashboard of the U-Haul as I buckle her into the passenger seat. She clutches a bag of snacks and will be Frank's little helper for the five-hour drive south, nearer to my childhood stomping grounds. Sammy is settled into his car seat behind me in the Subaru, wide-eyed and quiet like the day he was born, upstairs in the house we are now leaving. I follow the red taillights of the U-Haul and begin to cry, grateful for the pounding of rain on the roof. In the company of those tears, I allow mine to flow unimpeded.

I love my home. Why am I leaving it?

We are chasing a dream of a different sort—one Frank and I have cultivated for over a dozen years—a dream of living close to the Earth, with conscious interdependence and shared resources. A dream born from our nine-month foray in communal living during our first year together.

Since then we've held the flame, year after year, meeting after meeting, hoping to one day create communal nirvana. Sparks and enduring friendships were initiated, but never with enough fuel to ignite a fire for an intentional community here in the Adirondacks. When our dearest friends and allies left the area to live and work in a community downstate, we read the writing on the wall. We licked our wounds of weariness and disappointment and started looking for a place for ourselves.

Our gaze settled on Trilogy, a Camphill Community serving people with special needs, located downstate, within an hour's drive from my mom and four of my sisters. At the urging of a wise friend, we did not sell our house, but found renters—a young couple, who fell in love with our home. Before signing the lease, we added a clause—at their request—giving them first option to buy if we don't return. Tonight, they will sleep in *their* bed in *our* bedroom. And sit at *their* table in *our* kitchen.

This emotional dissonance, reminiscent of Goldilocks, befuddles me. The windshield wipers slap in rhythm and I collect myself, recalling Doug's gentle words as Frank and I walked out of our couples session the week before.

"Just remember to love each other, no matter what. If there is a problem for you there, it will show up in your dreams. Until then, I see no reason for you not to go. I have clients all over the country now. You're gonna find that phone sessions work great!"

Months earlier, we negotiated terms with Trilogy. Instead of a salary, all our living expenses would be covered in full, including a Waldorf education for the kids. Biweekly individual dream sessions and monthly couples sessions with Doug are also written into our financial agreement. Trilogy readily agreed, as they were in desperate need of stable house parents *and* someone to manage the market garden. Frank and I fit the bill and were seen as "an excellent catch," a fellow housemother told me, a few weeks later.

Before we walked out the door, Doug placed a hand on each of our shoulders; Frank and I reached for each other. Together, we formed a triangle—a symbolic moment before departing for Trilogy Camphill. Doug's eyes seemed even brighter than normal as he said, "Maybe you can help to bring *the work* to that area. Seems like it's a hotbed for spiritual seekers."

The idea that we could help *the work* flourish eased some of our angst about leaving the area just as momentum was building. Jenny was co-authoring a book about *the work* with Doug, while Pearl's husband, who has computer know-how and business sense, was starting a website. It was time to let the world know about this revolutionary work.

"It'll be good to be close to Mom, my sisters, and all your cousins," I say to myself and Sammy, who remains silent. Hours later, I turn my attention to a house with twice the square footage and twice the inhabitants as the one we left behind. As housemother, my responsibilities have multiplied to include one co-worker and three "friends," a loving term for individuals with special needs, to whom our lives are now dedicated. Everyone is so kind, welcoming us with cards, delicious food, helping hands, and big smiles.

ꝋ

I watch from my new kitchen window, hands immersed in the warm water of post-dinner dishes, as Frank walks down to the garden to inspect the long, rambling rows that feed the village's seventy people. Hand in hand, Layla and Sammy accompany him. I smile and chat with my lovely, introverted housemate and helper.

Once dishes are done, we walk to the barn to visit the small herd of six cows who are gentled in this nourishing environment. The farmer introduces me to Sigunny, the matriarch of the herd. I'm delighted to learn that my weekly schedule includes two morning milkings.

❦

I sit at the head of the table with eight bowls stacked on my left and a huge pot of steaming corn chowder in front of me. We bow our heads in blessing, thanking the many hands that brought this food to our table: Frank's garden crew for the onions, corn, and potatoes; the farmers for the milk and cream; and the bakery for the bread and hand-churned butter. Frank sits at the far end of the table, and Layla and Sammy are inserted between friends and co-workers—one big, happy family.

I cook, I clean, I teach life skills to my new housemates, celebrating our interdependence. I sit in many meetings. Before long, I stop trying to find my kids after school, trusting they are somewhere safe, at one of the houses or playing outdoors with their gaggle of friends.

Adjusting to this new life, one golden thread remains constant: *the work*. Doug delivers on his promise—phone sessions are even more effective than in-person. My one-hour sessions feel more focused. Sometimes we end early. Perhaps I'm finally beginning to "get" *the work*. I am breaking through to true feelings, instead of being trapped in old emotions riddled with pathology.

The physical distance and demands of our new positions make it difficult to participate in the organizing that's taking place up north. A seed is sprouting into the new Center for Transformational Learning (CTL). A graceful logo is created, along with a website with an email registry for people committed to becoming leaders in *the work*. Through CTL, a sacred container is forming for students to be "witnesses to self and others while outing pathology, practicing honesty, and being present to oneself and the divine." Anyone who works with Doug and agrees to the practice of "outing pathology" is invited to participate. I eagerly sign up. Membership also requires writing with transparency and honesty about one's inner work and reading each other's emails. I start writing and reading, and hop in my car whenever I can to drive four hours north to attend two-hour meetings. I nap in my car after meetings, unable to ask for a couch to sleep on, believing it would be frowned upon. No one offers a place to stay, and I don't know how to ask.

My psyche is stretched between my two worlds, untethered. By pulling up stakes and leaving the mountains, I've severed myself from my community and from my home. Home. I'd felt the first embodied sensation of "home" when I moved to the Adirondacks at nineteen years old, for what I'd thought would be only a couple weeks. But fresh air cleared the shadows from my head and clarified for me, in no uncertain terms, that I was where I belonged. Those mountains, I learned, were not part of the Catskills *or* the Appalachian chain. They are new mountains, still growing faster than erosion wears them away. The mountains spoke to me and accompanied my young adult years as I taught preschool, worked odd jobs, and lived with a sense of joyful adventure and ease.

I felt that sense of home again when I first entered what would become our backyard in Timberland. A towering tamarack, guardian white pines, and steadfast maples sang sweet harmonies as my feet sank into the soft grass for the first time. I knew it then, heeded the call, set down roots, and started a family there. But I'd given that up for our dream of intentional community. True grit and perseverance had become our motto, leading us to manifest our ideals for community living, come hell or high water.

༄

Morning milking has become a nodal point in my week, providing an opportunity to focus on my dream homework, and space to feel my true feelings. Every Monday and Thursday mornings, I slip out of the house before dawn, leaving breakfast responsibilities to Frank.

I nestle my head into Sigunny's side, my butt resting on the three-legged milking stool. I've gone back in time, milking by hand. My head rests in Sigunny's warmth, and I remember my homework: "Feel the insecurity, and notice when you go into your arrogance—the bravado hides your vulnerable self, which is your true self."

I take a deep breath as milk zings into the bucket, my hands pulsing in steady rhythm. My exhale whistles as I feel insecurity creeping in. Bravado has melted and I am in unfamiliar territory. *Have I made a mistake by moving here?!?*

Where is home? What is home? I feel lost, separated from all that was so familiar, so warmly "me." I left my hearth by choice, but I didn't anticipate just how vulnerable I would feel. Each day, I wake in a strange house and walk strange paths, desperate to feel at home. I had not realized just how comfortable my home of the last ten years had been for me.

From afar, my mountain home feels like my favorite dress. I am naked without it. I feel like a foreigner here, an imposter. I miss my home, miss my friends, miss seeing Doug in person. I feel incompetent, scared.

Doug says, "You feel what you have always felt, but covered up with years of skillful bravado." How many times have I said "I can do it"? I *can* do anything that takes me away from my own quaking heart, that keeps me stuck in pathology. I weep with the relief of feeling. I weep with relief of feeling honest.

Sigunny stands patiently as my head gently bumps up and down in quiet sobs. The bucket stands nearly full beneath her sagging udder. Milking's over.

I wonder if I am finally experiencing the difference between emotions and feelings, as Doug had tried to teach me in my first session, eight years ago. After my morning of weeping with Sigunny, I feel lighter, more present. I set about my day with acceptance of our decision to live here.

Camphill life is intense and wonderful in many ways. Our kids appear happy. Frank loves managing the garden. I'm okay with the cooking, cleaning, and caring for people who live with us. I like being able to call the maintenance man when the doorknob breaks, instead of trying to do it myself or nagging Frank to fix it. I don't have to worry about paying bills. We enjoy our Thursday evenings—our official time off—when our co-workers cover the dinner and bedtime duties. On those evenings, we go out to dinner as a family—just the four of us. We have fun checking out new restaurants. Wasabi, a low-key Japanese restaurant at the top of Main Street, is our favorite. Community living has so many benefits. Life is good. I start to wonder if maybe I could do this for a long time. Perhaps this *is* our destiny.

In mid-January, Trilogy begins its annual assessment of need. All house parents are asked to make commitments for the coming fiscal year, which runs July–June. Frank and I figure our first six months went pretty well, and decide to say "yes" to another year. The couple renting our house is eager to sign another lease.

"Remember, we want first option to buy if you are going to sell," they remind us. It's helpful to know the people living in our home love being there, supporting us to dive deeper into community life.

A few months after making our commitment to stay another year, Frank and I have an encounter with a bottle of vanilla that changes everything. It was a simple request.

I need vanilla for baking, and Frank loves vanilla on his morning yogurt. The price has sky-rocketed after a blight in Madagascar damaged the crop, so I ask Frank to discreetly add vanilla to his bowl in the kitchen, rather than bringing the bottle to the breakfast table, where eight people of varying fine-motor skills and abilities are likely to overuse it. I think he agrees.

The next morning, however, Frank brings the vanilla to the table and blurts, "I love vanilla!" And, of course, everyone wants some. The bottle empties in no time. I am stunned and humiliated—filled with anger, shame, and hurt. I leave the table, flee to my bedroom, and cry. I'm vaguely cognizant that this is an over-reaction, but floodgates open and there is no stopping the deluge of feelings.

The vanilla episode cracks me open, throws wide a door I cannot close, showing me the inequity in our marriage. I believed I was a liberated woman, married to a man as dedicated to equality, feminism, and reciprocity as I am. But a veil has lifted and laid bare the truth: I have followed Frank's passion and am now stuck in a stereotypical life binding me to a house that overwhelms me. A house where I am losing sight of my own children while I tend to other people's needs. A house where my husband appears for meals at the far end of a long table, while we become more and more estranged. I am losing my family to the ideals and glitter of community life. I cannot dare say this out loud, lest I appear ungrateful. Lest I disturb an apple cart so enticing, so alluring. I feel trapped. A tsunami of pain has crashed onto a thin shoreline and suddenly, our marriage is fragile.

My life tilts in an eerie parallel to a decision my mother made, years ago. She'd followed my father's desire to leave his stable office job for country living and farm life, which eventually lead to bankruptcy and divorce after twenty-one years and seven kids. Familial patterns now tug at my apron strings. The Earth beneath me shifts, as it did when I was sixteen years old and my mother told me we needed to go for a drive.

☙

With my learner's permit in hand, I sit in the driver's seat of the Chevy, as Mom twists her hands nervously beside me. We turn left onto Sunset Trail, where she asks me to pull over. There, she tells me, "Your dad and I are getting a divorce."

These words do not make sense. This happened to other families—not our family. We were a farm family. We endured hardship. I could not believe her words, until the silence that stretched between us shouted the truth: I was now in one of "those" families.

"Do you want me to drive home?" she asked. The sun had set beyond the horizon, darkness encroaching. I wanted to prove I could do it.

"I'll drive," I said, shaking. But the headlights created a tunnel, and try as I might to push it away, the dark was pressing down on me from all sides. I couldn't breathe. I pulled over, pushed the gear into park, and collapsed.

Sometimes, truth will not be muscled over.

☙

Frank and I have *fifteen months* to finish our commitment at Trilogy. We begin to talk honestly, reckoning with our marital difficulties in a new way. Doug helps us through couples sessions over the phone, video-conferencing not yet commonplace.

We look down the double-barreled gun of divorce and broken family, and dig deep to rekindle our marriage, unaware of the larger web we are becoming even more entangled in.

Retreat High

Summer, 2004

I HADN'T PLANNED ON ASKING Dad and LeAnne to watch
the kids so I can attend the CTL retreat. In fact, I don't have to—they
offer. For months leading up to it, I assumed I'd miss this inaugural
event, because Frank will be out of town at the Soul's Awakening
seminar—his anthroposophical training. I feel a pang every time I
read a retreat-update email or look at the glossy brochure. How can
I miss it?

I try not think about it.

The first stage of construction for the main retreat center is
complete. A glorious barn-like structure with a commercial kitchen;
large, open floor plan for meeting and dining; a loft for sleeping; and
a wide porch with mountain views now stands. Throughout the year
leading up to this event, thousands of volunteer hours have gone
into planning, developing, cleaning, and now offering the first public
retreat. The paint barely dry, the venue stands ready for spiritual
seekers and dreamers to arrive at what we fondly call "The Farm."

I'm not even sure where the name came from—no farming ever took place there; the soil is too shallow at that elevation. I suppose we farm spirit—turning over the compost of our psyches, weeding out pathology, growing our devotion to the divine, and harvesting our true calling in the world.

In the years to come, Frank and I will attend many retreats together. Hundreds of people will travel from all directions in summer, autumn, and winter to wind their way up the narrow mountain pass to The Farm, season after season. Before long, we find ourselves driving and flying long distances, following Doug to retreat centers all over the country, even overseas. But, currently, I am trying not to make a big deal about Frank leaving for *his* retreat, when I will miss CTL's.

"I'll be fine—I get to be at Mole End!" I tell him on the way to the airport. I force cheerfulness and chat about how much fun we will have with Dad and LeAnne at their rustic camp, a *Wind in the Willows* prototype. A couple hours southwest of Timberland, I muse out loud about maybe including a visit to friends before realizing everyone I would want to see will be at the CTL retreat.

Last summer, Layla crafted a birchbark sign with LeAnne's help, and held it up proudly—"MOLE END," it read, its letters perfectly askew—before nailing it to a tree at the top of the steep driveway that leads down to the rustic cedar camp.

The word "camp" was not in my family's vocabulary. We never went to camp, much less had such a place to go to, until Dad married LeAnne. As adults, with our own children in tow, we are now invited to Mole End's quiet refuge. This wild lakeside haven is nestled among towering cedar, hemlock, and white birch that stretch to catch the sunlight. The soil is thin, and boulders half-covered in lichen are scattered through the woods and along the path to the swimming dock on one side of camp, the boat dock on the other. Loon Lake is a jewel amongst many in the Adirondacks, a lake of seemingly endless length. Its wilderness is preserved, except on weekends, when noisy motorboats approach the property, then slow to navigate the narrow channel a stone's throw from the dock.

This year, I get to spend time there with Layla and Sam. Relieved to have a break from Trilogy, I relax in Mole End's embrace, drifting off to sleep with the smell of cedar and the gentle lapping of waves outside my window. Before bed, I must have been pining—or outright complaining—about not being able to attend the first-ever CTL retreat, because I am startled the next morning when LeAnne offers to keep the kids. Trembling, I dial Jenny's number on the rotary phone that hangs on the kitchen wall.

"Is there room for me? I'd like to come to the retreat tomorrow."

I hover close to the kitchen wall, coiled telephone cord wrapping around my legs, knowing the registration deadline was a week ago. The ancient phone line crackles, muffling her answer. My voice breaks when I ask again.

I'm aware of the scrutiny I will be under for registering at the last minute. By now, I know that asking for special consideration is most likely motivated by my pathology, my arrogance. I can hear Doug lamenting about how difficult it is to keep CTL "clean." We hold pathology at bay when we abide by Doug's guidelines, which come to him from the Divine. I'm breaking a rule by registering late, but that does not stop me from asking.

While the idea of "camp" was not familiar in our family, independence was. It had not occurred to me to ask my family to watch my kids so I could attend the retreat. I was aware that other families had grandparents who are happy to keep their grandkids for a night or two, but I didn't think of it until LeAnne offered. *That's how I will explain it to Doug,* I decide. There is no question, though, that my late registration will be perceived as lack of commitment to *the work.*

Years earlier, I forgot to pay Doug for a session, and he taught me how my "forgetting" was really a passive-aggressive attack on *the work*, and ultimately on Doug, too. "It's your inner resistance to *the work*," Doug growled at me. "You're letting pathology have a heyday. What you're really saying is that you don't want to pay me, that *you* know better than I do, and *I* should pay *you!*"

I was horrified to hear this, tried to interject that I'd simply forgotten my checkbook, but he continued. "It's dangerous, Gerette. You think it's a small, insignificant act, but it's not. Pathology wants to take you down and wants to sabotage all the inner work you have done. You've got to root out this kind of behavior!"

"Yes!" This time, there is no mistake. Jenny, whom I admire and fear, goes on to tell me arrival details. "You've missed the registration deadline, but no worries, just bring a check with you," she says cheerfully.

I rummage through my purse to make sure I have my checkbook, and put it on top of the dresser with my keys, where I'll be sure not to forget it.

The next morning, feeling like a kid released early from school, I kiss Layla and Sammy goodbye, grateful for Dad and LeAnne at their side. I am euphoric, driving solo through the High Peaks wilderness to the far north. I'm glad to be on my own, to have a break from the kids and from Frank. It's hard work, repairing a marriage. My heart soars as each turn of the highway reveals more mountain views, boreal forests, and elevation gains and losses before the steady incline to my final destination.

This is my first weekend away from both kids *and* husband. My drive is sprinkled with inner affirmations: "The Animus wants this for me." "This is the beginning of CTL moving out into the world, and I get to be a part of it!" "I am being supported to become more and more the person God wants me to be."

I practically fly to the mountain retreat center and arrive ahead of schedule, halfway up little-known Monroe Mountain.

Before the pandemic of 2020, I read an article in *Business Insider* about "wellness retreats." Katie Warren, the journalist, wrote, "Wealthy travelers [. . .] are spending their money on 'wellness summits,' spirituality retreats, and resorts that focus on health and self-care. Wellness retreats have become a huge industry, expected to grow to $920 *billion* by 2022."[4]

I'm pretty sure her statistics *didn't* include the CTL's of the world—of which there are many. CTL, as well as countless other small self-help groups, function independent of the large wellness retreats featured in Warren's article. Humans devote a staggering amount of resources to flee from the mundane in order to feel good—or to feel terrible, doing "deep work." Everyday cults can be just as slick as wellness retreats at capitalizing on the promise of redemption, enlightenment, and freedom from everyday drudgery.

Walking to The Farm from the parking area, I feel that sensation again—I am home. Light pours into the meeting space from the cathedral window, pooling in the open expanse where people are starting to gather. The smell of newly sawn pine mixes with the savory aroma of a bubbling cauldron of pulled pork—Doug's specialty.

When I see Jenny at the registration table, dread interrupts my reverie, and I panic. My mind races. Where is my checkbook? My heart freezes as I realize it is still on the dresser at Mole End. I grabbed the spare keys from the glove box, so I didn't have to return to the house after saying goodbye to the kids.

Shit.

Shame rises. *This is your pathology. You are so arrogant—to register at the last minute, and then arrive without payment. Who do you think you are?*

When I gather the courage to approach Jenny, she scrunches her nose and tells me to talk with Doug. I feel like an alien and assure her I will mail a check first thing Monday.

Controlling group codes define the terms of engagement. These terms are often unrealistic and defy what it is to be human. Take one step too far to the right, and a border collie swings in to nip at your heels. Stray off the path to the left, and he yelps you back in line. My loyalty is being stitched in place, making it easy to respond without taking a stand. Sure. I will tow Doug's line. If this is how I become enlightened, I'll do what it takes.

The lively chatter quiets to a murmur, then silence when Doug arrives. I move toward the large circle of participants, catching my breath as he welcomes us, my senses alert and tingling.

"Today is a new beginning for *the work*. We can be g-g-grateful for the Animus who brought us here." Doug stutters slightly and seems nervous. Many of us know he doesn't like speaking in groups, and we silently cheer him on.

Jenny announces our names, divided into small groups. I'm glad to be in her group, despite the shame of having forgotten my checkbook. It's an honor to be with her and others who, it seems to me, have status in *the work*. We go outside to the rough foundation of what will later become an elegant patio with expansive mountain views. Eight of us make ourselves comfortable using pillows, back jacks, and low folding chairs, circling close to each other.

Unbeknownst to me, Doug had asked a handful of people to write out their dreams before the retreat. Mona, the wife of an author from Berkeley, was one of the lucky ones. Status makes itself known through unconscious bias. A pecking order was being woven into the social fabric of CTL, consciously or not. To be fair, Doug never promised egalitarianism, but I doubt he was aware of the favoritism being established at this very first retreat.

We make informal introductions as we settle into our respective seats. This is the real work, where we act out a dream, psychodrama style. It will take another year of experimentation before several teachers have "instruction dreams," teaching us the sacred Branch Therapy that will become our trademark. For now, we have only each other, Jenny's grounded leadership, and our trust and willingness to show up for ourselves and each other.

When Doug approaches our group, we fall silent. He and Jenny whisper together for a few minutes, reading over Mona's dream, then Doug turns away from our group. We watch him walk toward the upper lean-to, where another group is meeting. Jenny leads us in a simple grounding exercise and describes how we are going to enact some dreams. "This is all an experiment," she says. "A sacred experiment. Let's see what happens."

Jenny reads Mona's first dream aloud:

I'm at a chaotic outdoor marketplace—noisy and bustling with activity. A man sits away from the action, hunched over, nearly hidden by his cloak.

At Jenny's invitation, several participants stand to play roles as shopkeepers, patrons, and rambunctious kids. "Who wants to be the man?" Jenny asks. A surge of energy fills me as I raise my hand. Jenny gestures for me to step into the center of our circle. I drape a shawl over myself and sit quietly, watching Mona. As she walks around, shopping and chatting with others, I—as the man in her dream—am riveted to every move she makes. When she glances at me, a deep longing to connect with her swells up out of nowhere. Jenny asks if I, the man, want to speak to Mona.

"I see your beauty in every step you take." I rise and my heart speaks. "I have been waiting for you. I am here for you."

Embodying the Animus in Mona's dream, I am filled with clarity. Words and gestures flow, moving Mona to tears. I am humbled.

We explore three dreams that day, awed by how much we absorb through each other's dreams. The power of this first experience fills me with vitality, stirring the flame of my past as a thespian in community theater, but this is richer and so much more meaningful. By focusing on our dreams and listening to the voices of the unconscious, we feel ourselves tapping into a world that stirs the soul.

"We'll have a bonfire at 'King's Corner' tonight!" Doug announces after dinner. "Let's celebrate. John will lead us in songs at the fire."

The sun is sinking behind us, and we trek an uneven path through the woods. We ascend far up Monroe Mountain as the light dims. We're greeted by a crackling bonfire in a wide, flat area deep in the forest. With his harmonica and mandolin, John starts us off with a familiar tune. We break into song. When we falter with the lyrics, John's voice keeps going. His musical repertoire is endless, and he carries the melody when the group wavers. When enough of us are secure with the tune, John's resonant tenor ventures off into harmonies, lending resonant depth to our campfire fun. In the pause between songs, the deep quiet of the woods speaks. I imagine squirrels, fox, deer, and moose bending their ears our way, curious, if not alarmed, at humans this high up. I picture the big cat whose telling tracks crossed mine in the snow, months earlier, during a women's group retreat in the cabin. A shiver runs up my spine.

The evening ends too soon, when Doug says it's time to head down to The Farm. I wonder, *why so early?* Perhaps Doug has detected someone drifting into pathology. Nonetheless, when Doug declares it's time to go, we go. I linger, helping to put out the fire and savoring the quiet of the woods returning to its natural sounds as the human voices descend.

"Thanks, John," I whisper, the dark settling around us. "This was such a special evening." John is one of few men in *the work* I feel easy with. We stragglers make our way down the ragged trail, following the bobbing flashlight beam. When we break free from the woods into the upper field, we whoop, seeing the soft glow of The Farm. Our new home. The spiritual home for *the work*. We switch off the flashlight and descend together, drinking in the silence.

Next morning, we gather in a large closing circle where several people from each group share testimony about the transformational experience of receiving Doug's guidance in acting out dreams. Doug's response is succinct and affirming.

"You all have your homework—it is your individual doorway to your soul. Remember to do it as much as you can. And if you want more of this up here"—he spreads his hands wide to include the land and everything The Farm has to offer—"come on back. We will have another retreat this winter."

On my drive back to Loon Lake, I am high on newfound intimacy, the joy of finding my tribe, and the power of connecting deeply with my soul-self. I find *the work* sacred and profound. I want more of it.

This high has faded by the time I have my next session with Doug, who berates me for the forgotten check. "This pathology is a pattern, Gerette. You've got to work harder and not let this crap pollute your work!"

At the end of a later retreat, Doug closes with a short lecture of warning. "When your soul has grown this much, this quickly, you have to be prepared for backlash. Pathology is going to raise its ugly head and challenge you to your core! It's going to start fighting hard, so you have to be prepared and fight it with your homework."

As time goes on, I learn to schedule a session with Doug within a few days after each retreat, to get extra help. I always need it. The homework we receive at a retreat is the distillation of our deepest inner work yet, with the greatest emotional intensity. It is infused with the dynamic exchange we embody with our fellow retreat-mates. Homework and ongoing guidance from Doug are our only defense against our pathology, which wants nothing more than to revert us to the un-evolved people we were before starting *the work*.

When we leave a retreat, we're motivated to do our homework with greater commitment. No matter what we are doing in our daily lives, we can pause, recall the specific homework prescription, and try to reconnect with the feelings we felt in our retreat circle. We are dedicated to this process—of conjuring our seminal retreat moment, twice a day or twice an hour, because we are told that the more we do it, the greater our inner growth. This is how we access connection with the Animus, with the divine forces that are our true support. If we are diligent with our homework, it could lead to further breakthroughs. Out of the unconscious, in the acting out of our dreams, we seek to gain new access to the reservoir of higher consciousness. Our retreat homework holds a higher frequency than our normal homework, and is referenced throughout the months, even years, to come. If dream homework provides stepping stones to inner growth, retreat homework is an island to return to, again and again.

According to the late psychiatrist, M. Scott Peck, group participation can be dangerous. He wrote, "Most people would rather be followers. ...there is a profound tendency for the average individual to emotionally regress as soon as he becomes a group member."[5] Regress? Yes, he claimed, like children looking for their parents.

Was our intelligence and capacity for discernment being

systematically dialed back by biological and tribal instincts? Did we become kids, believing the fairy dust of our homework would make us grow, and protect us from evil? We wielded our magical homework swords, ready to meet the world head on. *The work* intensified through retreats and became, for me at least, a kind of drug which I craved like a kid begging for more ice cream.

Rip and Return

Spring, 2005

SAMMY REACHES ON TIPTOES AND pulls *The Treasure*[6] off the bookshelf.

"This one, Mama."

I smile and remind him to pee before we start reading. His bare feet patter down the tile hallway, and I sit on his bed. Gazing out the small window from our basement suite, I watch the fading light cast gold onto the highest tree limbs.

I'm glad we moved our family into the basement of our Trilogy home, providing more privacy for the four of us. I needed the buffer. It's a beautiful life in many ways; Frank loves being the head gardener, and I feel guilty when I mention Timberland or the Adirondacks. Our marriage was shaken by "the vanilla episode," but with Doug's help our marriage has stabilized.

Sammy climbs onto his bed and I smile as we settle into our bedtime reading. *The Treasure* is one of my favorites. The story goes like this:

There is a poor man named Isaac who has a recurring dream about a treasure under the bridge at a king's palace in a faraway city. He travels to the bridge to discover it is guarded night and day. He goes there again and again, hoping to be able to look for the treasure.

One day, the captain of the guards asks him why he keeps showing up. Isaac tells him about his dream. The captain laughs and replies, "If I believed in dreams, I would go to the city where you came from and find a treasure under the stove in the house of a man named Isaac!"

Isaac set off for the long journey home, and lo and behold—he finds a great treasure under his stove. After sending a ruby to the captain, he builds a house of prayer. In the corner of this chapel, he places an inscription:

"Sometimes one must travel far to find that which is near."

I wipe a tear before it reaches my cheek and kiss Sammy goodnight. That night, Frank holds me as I quietly cry myself to sleep.

I wake the next morning: "Wow. I dreamt of Rip!"

Rip Van Aiken was one of a kind: a horse farmer, joke teller, fixer-upper, salt-of-the-earth man. When I was a kid, Rip would appear most days in our farm's kitchen, bringing with him a half-empty coffee mug and a joke. Rip brought us Duffy, the horse who thought he was a cow, who happily co-existed in barn and pasture with our herd of Holsteins. Rip and Duffy were bonded to each other as much as we were to both of them. We were grateful Rip had excuses to stop by so often. Not that he needed one. Rip happened by our place the evening of the cyclops.

Molly, our oldest and most reliable ewe, is due to lamb and hasn't returned to the shed for afternoon feeding. I am walking through the fields, looking for her before evening falls. Finally, I see her in the upper pasture, afterbirth trailing as she efficiently licks a lamb clean.

I am puzzled. Molly always has twins. Where was the other one? I scan the area and see it lying a few yards away in the tall grass. I approach, then freeze. The lamb has one large eye socket in the middle of its forehead, with two black eyeballs looking crazily toward, but through me.

I drop to the ground, kneeling beside this newborn creature. It's jaw is jutted forward and arched upward, wildly askance, but its male body is large and robust. I realize Molly is ignoring him, and know why. I wonder how to save him, picturing the awkwardness of bottle feeding and then raising him, a symbol of ovine resilience and human dedication. I could love him, I am sure. I rise and run as fast as I can to the house. Breathless, I tell Mom and Rip, and immediately start shaking.

Mom makes me hot cider with a shot of rum in it. Rip puts his warm hand on my shoulder before quietly heading out to the field to take care of it. Next morning, we agree this is the last year Molly will be bred.

❧

In the early morning light, Frank looks at me with tenderness. Just before we left the mountains, my mom called to let me know that Rip had died, with his wife and daughter by his side. I'd not seen Rip since I was a teenager, but felt bereft nonetheless. A world without Rip is an emptier world.

"Wow. What did you dream?" Frank asks. And I tell him:

I am at a country fair when Mom comes up to tell me she

*just saw Rip! I head in his direction and see him in the
distance with his daughter, as they attempt to get a small
hang glider in the air. I feel insecure, since I haven't seen
him in years, and wonder if he will recognize me. He sees
me and waves.*

*"Of course I recognize you!" he says, and swoops in
for a bear hug. He still sports his goofy smile and faded
beret, cocked sideways on his bald head. I tell him there
is so much to talk about. We look into each other's eyes. He
laughs and tells me I used to shave my legs when I was
only twelve years old.*

*I laugh and say, "That's funny. I don't shave them
now!"*

*Marge, his wife, arrives and I ask if they are still
living in Missouri.*

"No," she says. "We live in Timberland!"

"Timberland, PA?" I ask, surprised.

*"No. Timberland, New York!" she says. I am stunned
to realize they've been living so close to me, all these years.*

Doug taught that dreams about people who've died bear special
significance, and often bring a specific message to the dreamer. Frank
is quiet after hearing my dream. We cuddle until we both need to get
to work.

Throughout the day and the following weeks, I replay the dream
scene over and over in my mind. The jolt of energy I feel when Marge
says *"Timberland, New York!"* opens a floodgate. I miss Timberland.
I miss home. In my next session, Doug sees this dream as prophetic.

"The Animus wants you to return to Timberland, where you can be
a part of the new phase of *the work*. You have an important role here,
Gerette."

Hearing this, I swoon. I feel seen—acknowledged in a new way. After all the angst of deciding whether or not to leave Trilogy, Rip appearing in my dream *does* feel prophetic. Frank feels it too.

"Sometimes one must travel far to find that which is near."

Two years almost to the day of our leaving, we drive a U-Haul back up our driveway in Timberland, putting the glorified intentional community life behind us. Frank landed an excellent job working for the Office of Children and Family Services, and I will take the rest of the summer off to resettle our family before determining my next career step. I know I need something that allows me to participate fully in the burgeoning CTL organization.

I write an email to CTL members:

> My homework is to be with Rip and Marge, living in Timberland, to feel the sense of belonging, of being connected to the Animus and Anima who are here to love and guide me through this transition period. I am scared by the depth, honesty, integrity, and love I feel in the growing CTL community. I have awakened to the truthfulness of my heart connection with *the work*. In my present state of structures and ideals crumbling, it is the *only* thing I know for sure.

I unpack boxes and survey the changes since we left two years ago. A large spot of candle wax on the rug dismays me. I shudder to think what could have happened if it had caused a fire. I'd inherited that green wool rug from Mom.

The renters had installed a plywood cupboard door, replacing the hanging curtain under the sink, and I decide I like it enough to paint it. I think to myself, *Home sweet home. And what's best of all?* I muse quietly, *We are back just in time for the annual CTL retreat! I'd better figure out who will take care of the kids.*

After leaving Doug, a decade later, I pull *The Treasure* off the shelf, its pages weathered and worn, and imagine the captain of the guards in a new light: he looks at the foolish woman who kept returning to the brightly lit palace called *the work*, and says "Ha! If I believed in dreams, I would travel to Timberland and find a treasure under the hearth in the home of a woman named Gerette."

The treasure *is* our home and the land we have the privilege of stewarding. I sense an ancient relationship this land holds for me, reluctant as I have been to listen for its voice. I am grateful every day for its patience. I have strayed, been distracted, in the same way I sometimes neglect my own body by eating crappy food or not getting enough exercise.

Perhaps there is a kind of pairing of resonance that happens when one's body vibrates with a particular piece of land, like finding a soul mate. Body-for-body, saying, "Yes. I recognize you. We speak the same language. We have danced together before."

Like most courtships, the journey to maturity is not a straightforward path, but one with many turns, bumps, bridges, and dead ends. At long last, the wanderer returns home, aged and wizened. All along, the Earth stays steady.

Our return to Timberland marked the half-way point in my eighteen-year odyssey with Doug.

The Biz

THE DALRYMPLE BOYS WERE OBSESSED with frogs. When I was a kid, we'd meet up after school at "the pit"—an old gravel yard with a small pond. One day, Calvin, the middle boy about my age, told me how they took some frogs home and put them in a pot of water on the stove.

"Ya shoulda' seen 'em! Climbin' on top of each other to get outta that pot!" Hands flapping in excitement, he went on to describe how, as the water heated, the frogs' movements slowed until they boiled to death. The Dalrymple boys squealed, delighted with their experiment, and my stomach turned into a knot.

Authors Jamie Sams and David Carson revere Frog in their book, *Medicine Cards*, wherein they write, "Frog teaches us to honor our tears, for they cleanse the soul."[7]

As a kid, hanging out with my hardscrabble neighbors, I could never have imagined that, one day, *I* would be in hot water, having lost my instinct to get out. The frog-self wants to get the heck out of the pot—any pot—and back into Nature. Survival compels them—

and us—to act. A warming pot, however, entices me to stay awhile.

≥

"I'm done saving the world," I promise Adelaide over the phone. I watch Sam from my living room bay window as he hauls his rusty dump truck to the sandbox. Adelaide is my new friend, met during our stint at Trilogy, but it feels like I've known her for decades, rather than just two years.

She and I bonded over the creation of a gingerbread church for the school fundraiser. Her cabin was her refuge from a crumbling relationship, and home for her two kids—and me, for a couple hours twice a week through the month of November.

I'd steal away from my duties at Trilogy to focus on the structural integrity of slabs of gingerbread and sugar paste while we built a lasting friendship. Adelaide was reconciling her desire to become a priest, while severing ties with the father of her kids. As we erected edible church walls, our conversation pivoted from "What color lifesavers should we melt for windows?" to "Well, the church frowns on people who have children out of wedlock—but it's not going to stop me from trying." (It didn't stop her. She was ordained several years later and called to a large Episcopal church out West.)

We built a steeple and bell tower, and pasted slivered almonds, one by one, for the shingled roof. A tiny brass bell in the steeple was the perfect final touch to our masterpiece—except, brass wasn't edible and therefore disqualified us from the contest. Nonetheless, our monument fetched one of the top bids in the auction.

Frank and the kids and I returned home a couple of weeks ago, and I need to figure out what to do for work once the kids are back in school. Scanning job openings for teachers, managers at care facilities, and front desk positions leaves me empty and flat. Nothing moves me.

"I need work that I don't bring home with me at the end of the day—practical work that pays *really* well!" I sigh at the hopeless thought.

"Seems to me, you have two choices," Adelaide says in her I've-been-through-this-ringer-before voice. "House painting or cleaning." She chuckles. "And you know me—I'd only have one choice." I'd spent enough time in her house to know that cleaning was *not* her thing.

"I'm a crappy painter," I say, stepping outside to check on Sammy. "Cleaning it is!"

Hanging up the phone, I feel lighter. Adelaide was right. Cleaning for a living is honest labor that I won't worry about at the end of the day. I smile—if the only purpose of the two-year Trilogy ordeal was for me to find Adelaide, it was worth it. Then, I wonder how to start a cleaning business.

Later that day I run into Kelly, a mom from North River, at the grocery store. I hadn't seen her since she was thrown from a horse the summer we left for Trilogy. We're catching up in the baking aisle when I tell her about my newly-hatched entrepreneurial idea, and her eyes brighten.

"You have to check out The Clean Team!" she gushes with surprising sincerity. "Jeff Campbell saved my life!" Kelly describes how healing from traumatic brain injury after the horse incident required her to break down everyday tasks into specific steps. The Clean Team does this. I'm curious, and promise her I'll look them up. I grab a bag of Ghirardelli chocolate chips and head to the produce aisle.

Turns out, Kelly is spot-on. I discover that, not only did nerdy Jeff Campbell craft a system of efficient cleaning, he also created a how-to guide for starting a cleaning business, which I order immediately.

According to Doug, God likes entrepreneurs. He gushes, like Kelly did, when I tell him my plan. Overnight, I gain confidence in my new career. Rolling up my sleeves, I am propelled by Doug's encouragement. This feels like synergy—my inner life intensifying through what I do in the world. I feel ready for the call.

❧

John J. is at the door, he is going out but needs his license. He playfully picks up my purse and says "I'll take this one!"

I take out my wallet and toss it to him, saying, "Take it."

He looks at me intently and says, "No. I won't do that."

I realize that I was ready to give my identity away!

"Right," I say. "You are you, and I am I!"

Doug tells me to see this as a warning dream. As I enter the business world, I need to make sure I don't give myself away by undercharging and overworking. Doug talks about my dream with others in the CTL community who are working on various start-ups. John is beginning his handyman business around this time—hearing my dream is affirming for him, too. As it turns out, I do have a tendency to undercharge for my work. I take lessons from this dream, again and again. Even so, I am making good money and working hard.

Being engaged in CTL work is equally thrilling. The mentoring program is demanding, but my inner work, CTL, and my new business are interwoven and mutually supportive, with Doug as my guide. Every session begins with Doug cheerfully asking, "How's 'The Biz' going?"

At first, it's easy to respond, "Great!"

There is a point in the cool of the northern springtime, just after garden beds have been raked out, when everything looks seductively tidy. Under the Earth's surface, a storm is brewing, ready to burst forth on the first warm days. This lull before the growth separates true gardeners from wannabes. It takes chutzpa to stay the gardening course here. If you miss a beat, you're in the weeds in no time. I learn the same is true for running a business.

I am flabbergasted by how easy it is to get customers. Lots of people don't like to clean and will happily pay good money for someone else to wash their floors, scrub their toilets, and take out their garbage. My schedule fills quickly, and the calls keep coming in. Saying "no" does not come easily to me, so I overschedule.

Within six months, I become a workaholic.

The Guru Papers: Masks of Authoritarian Power offers a cogent lens on the relationship between authoritarian systems and addiction.[8] Authors Joel Kramer and Diana Alstad claim that people with addiction often possess what they call an "inner authoritarian" who drives a value system that is impossible to live up to. This self-defeating inner critic is fueled by top-down social systems. We constantly strive for something we will never achieve: the perfection our leader—or our inner authoritarian—endorses. We will not achieve it, because it is unrealistic. Unattainable. Addiction becomes one way to manage the stress resulting from having severed from the gentler, more realistic worldview that accepts the limitations of being human and celebrates multiplicity—the kindness of humankind.

Instead, I become a driven woman. Before long, I am in the weeds with no billing system, back aches, and I hardly ever see my kids. At Doug's urging I consider hiring help, but think of our accountant, who issued me a stern warning.

Walking with her up the stairs to her office one day, I announced my intention to start the cleaning business. She stopped mid-step, looked directly at me, and said, "I would think long and hard before hiring employees." I didn't voice my counter argument, that most people in business didn't have spiritual guidance, like I did.

"The Animus will guide you. You have so much potential. The natural state of the universe is growth. Vitality infused with God's love wants to grow." I listen keenly to Doug's wisdom. "The danger is when it gets polluted. You have to watch for pathology, because it can look a lot like God's wishes. I can help you, and of course, your dreams will help you to know what's what."

I make my first hires—a young couple. I train them, and love working with them. The three of us create a team that kicks ass in any house, no matter how big or how dirty. I feel the power of efficiency, Clean Team-style, grateful for Jeff Campbell's business guide. *This* is vitality.

In the garden, you might get one bed weeded to perfection, the seedlings come in, and you sigh in relief. In the time it takes to sigh, though, while gazing out across the fields at the setting sun, a jungle forms in the next bed. My current jungle is organization. I need management help in the office, *and* I need someone who can clean when needed.

"Hire Marie! She's looking for work," Doug suggests. Marie and I fell out of touch after North River Waldorf School closed its doors, just after Sammy was born. She'd moved back to Quebec for a while but family dynamics became toxic, so she returned to New York and was trying to pick up the pieces of her life. The opportunity to reconnect with her, and the fact that she's in *the work* and joined CTL, is too good to be true. I trust Doug's suggestion and hire Marie for part-time work, no need for an interview.

She quickly becomes my right-hand woman. She helps in the office *and* is an excellent cleaner. We do homework check-ins every day—reflecting on what we each need to do to stay in alignment with our inner work—while cleaning or managing the office. We become sisters. I see her vulnerabilities and want to support her growth—both practically, in the world, and inwardly, in her soul work. If God likes entrepreneurs, He must be smiling upon this partnership.

We work hard. We laugh. We cry together. And every month, we meet with Doug so he can coach us to become the best possible partners—committed to truly working *the work*—in the world and in our hearts. These monthly business sessions are a financial priority for my cleaning company in the same way our individual and couples sessions are a priority for Frank and me. I feel deeply supported by this multifaceted approach. The Biz is flourishing.

Doug was a master at quid pro quo—I'll pay you to scrub my kitchen floor and you come to my retreats. He had business dealings with many of his clients: John was his personal handyman. Kit sewed drapes for his wife. Willy did the plumbing.

Doug provided his version of therapy, but he was not licensed, not bound to any "bothersome" standards. Doug was free to interact with his clients however he wanted. My partnership with Marie guaranteed five or more paid sessions for him each month, but I didn't see Doug's game at the time. Unaware of the deal, the cards were stacked against us.

Marie's back goes out. The cleaning is too hard on her body, and it's getting to me, too. Sporadic shooting pain radiates down my legs when I vacuum more than four hours a day. I cannot keep up with my CTL job, or reading and writing emails. I come to the painful realization that I need to prioritize my business right now, and leave CTL. Doug reminds me, "We have an open-door policy. You can leave and return whenever you want." I cry when I write my "leaving CTL" email:

I am leaving now, so I can return in a few months with

greater clarity and commitment. I will, of course, continue working with Doug personally, professionally, and doing couple's work. I am only stepping back from my dedication to promoting CTL out in the world right now. I WILL BE BACK!

It's time to hire another cleaner, so I'm checking the references of a young man who's applied for the position. I call Kim Hanson, who owns and operates a twenty-year-old cleaning company in Southbury, forty minutes south of Timberland. She laughs out loud when I ask about him.

"I can't believe he had the nerve to tell you that he worked for me! I fired him because he was stealing shit from my customers!" Kim exclaims.

I like chatting with her, and we decide to meet for coffee at the Rail Station, one of the longest-running breakfast and lunch places in the Adirondacks. We have a blast comparing notes, laughing and complaining about the joys and struggles of life in the cleaning world. She has over a dozen employees and a few hundred customers, but only works part-time, running the office.

"I'm so jealous," I say as we're wrapping up our conversation. "But you give me hope that I could get there too!"

"Do you want to buy my business?" Kim blurts. "I've been doing this for twenty years and I'm tired of it. I want to garden and make stained glass."

I'm speechless.

A few days later, Marie and I have a business coaching session with Doug. It's a sticky, hot July day, and we sit in the gazebo in his backyard. Marie is feeling very low.

"How's The Biz?" Doug starts as usual, looking at Marie, then me, and settling his eyes back on Marie. A rooster crows, even though it's the middle of the day.

"I can't keep doing this much cleaning." She chokes back tears. "And I can't survive on fifteen hours a week." She knows I can't afford to pay for more office hours. But the idea of her leaving makes me want to cry, too. Then, almost in a trance, I describe my conversation with Kim Hanson, and as the words leave my mouth, I sense electricity in the air. "She asked if I wanted to buy her cleaning business." My body is erect, my voice steady and clear. "Perhaps this is the answer."

Doug leaps off his chair and paces. "Yes! Can't you feel it? This is what God wants. He is guiding you to buy the company. Marie can be the office manager, and you can have more time at home, like you want! Yes! This is how God works!"

Frank and I schedule an emergency couples session. He is skeptical, but not closed to the idea. It doesn't take much convincing, and Frank offers that he still has $25,000 from his inheritance that can be used as a down-payment.

When I ask Kim how much she wants for the business, she says $100,000. I can't conceive coming up with that kind of money. But when I tell Doug, he advises, "Don't dicker with her. God doesn't work that way. Look—she devoted twenty years to this business. She deserves it."

Frank writes out a check for $25,000. I sign the legal documents for transfer of ownership, plus a $75,000 promissory note agreeing to pay Kim five hundred dollars a week, plus 3 percent interest until the loan is paid.

In one of my earliest sessions, Doug drew three concentric circles, showing me his model for healthy boundaries in relationships. In the center circle was me and God; Frank and the kids were in the next circle; friends, family, and close colleagues were in the next one; and everyone else was outside that third circle.

That sketch became a reference point for me, because I tend to over-give in relationships that are outside the third circle, leaving less of me for those who matter most. This was one of the helpful lessons I learned from Doug. Two decades later, however, it occurs to me: Doug wormed his way into my center circle through his unscrupulous teachings. *When did that happen? And how?*

Indoctrination is like that pot of water on the Dalrymple boys' stovetop, gradually approaching the boiling point. Doug became God sometime between the warmth and the rising steam.

Mentoring Mind

Summer and Fall, 2005

"NOT EVERYONE CAN HANDLE THE intensity of it, but I think you're ready," Doug tells me.

"Sign me up!" I reply. I barely lasted two months away from CTL, before returning with renewed commitment.

It was the mentoring program that motivated me to come back. Doug paired me with Sandy, a dark-haired, doe-eyed young woman who'd waited on me many times at the Rail Station. I'm surprised to learn she's been in *the work* for over a decade, too. Her quiet, ethereal nature intrigues me.

Before my first meeting with Sandy, I pore over the program's guidelines, studying each of the nine steps. The first three detail the communication process and requirements for being accepted into the mentoring program. CTL membership, necessary for enrollment, requires members to take on jobs of increasing responsibility and time commitments, based on their level of membership, the member's skills, and the needs of the organization. A membership handbook identifies various positions and committees, but they are constantly shifting to meet both organizational and personal growth needs. All jobs are assigned by Doug and can be changed at any time in order to preserve the integrity of both the organization and the individual's inner work. (Power dynamics operate best when the one in charge is an all-knowing master who behaves erratically and whose decisions are unpredictable. In this security vacuum, the lesser ones scramble to find meaning in the greater one's actions, unaware the goalposts are moving.)

The next three steps of the mentoring program's guidelines describe how to schedule and identify roles. Each participant is assigned two or three partners with whom to alternate the role of mentor and mentee in separately scheduled, in-person meetings.

Step seven is the crucible work:

"The mentee describes an example of how their pathology was triggered within the sacred container of CTL. The trigger can arise from a class, during a retreat, in response to homework, or most importantly, in reaction to their CTL job. The mentor sits in loving attention, witness to how the pathology is manifesting. The mentor's only actions are to ask clarifying questions and takes notes."

That's it. So simple. So powerful. Learn about pathology from the master: pathology itself.

"The goal of the CTL Mentoring Program is to become more conscious of our reactions and our projections *in action*. We will learn there is no separation between our inner work and the mentoring program. *Everything* is fuel for our capacity to scour the depths of our souls, to root out pathology, and to prevent it from polluting the sacred container of *the work*."

The eighth step is simply to meet again and switch mentor/mentee roles, with the caveat that meetings are scheduled within one week of each other. In addition to Sandy, I am assigned to two new CTL members. That makes six meetings every two weeks. This commitment makes me breathless with excitement. I believe I am being offered extraordinary support through the mentoring program, at no cost. Five years later, after leaving CTL, I learn the real cost of my involvement.

The ninth and final step of the mentoring guidelines is the engine that makes it all possible:

"Both mentor and mentee review their mentoring sessions with master analyst, Doug. This is essential so that any necessary adjustments can be made before your next cycle of meetings. By bringing everything back to the master analyst, you are assured of a tight container where your progress can be tracked, giving pathology less room to move around. It may be necessary to schedule additional sessions."

And yes, we had to pay for all sessions with Doug.

I complete this cycle twice with Sandy and once each with two other members, and I love it. I don't feel good about dashing out the door as soon as Frank gets home from work, or about getting a sitter for the kids so I can go straight from a cleaning job. I want to hear more about how Frank's new job is going. But, between the mentoring program, my burgeoning cleaning business, and other CTL commitments, I believe I'm finally learning to prioritize my soul work.

I feel the power of mentoring: it's a loving process, sitting with allies in *the work*, excavating our psyches before a witness. It's thrilling—we chase the pathology dragon, grab it by its tail, and slap it down. *Ha! There you are!* It's vulnerable—we open our hearts to each other as we search for the inner demons that seek to undermine our growth. We are pathology hunters, bringing all evidence of our malaise back to our leader for further insight, grateful to Doug for being what we playfully call "our bullshit police."

Doug gets frustrated with my mistakes. He says I'm taking the rules too literally, and urges me to ask more questions. I take this to heart and have what I think is a breakthrough session with Sandy. I bring my notes and several questions to my session with Doug, excited to learn more.

I step into his office and am greeted with a scowl. My heart sinks. Sandy had a session earlier in the day, and told Doug she was "super uncomfortable" with how I treated her. Doug asks me if I even know the mentoring guidelines.

My mind whirrs: of course I know the mentoring process . . . *but was my pathology running the show while I was mentoring Sandy?*

I'd been primed to believe any problem was my fault. I was about to learn the tenth step of the mentoring guidelines—the unwritten one: Brace yourself if your partner speaks to Doug first. Sincerity, loyalty, dedication to the truth—all qualities to strive for, unless they are turned against you, manipulating reality. The tenth step is about gaslighting and dissociation. They go hand in hand.

"Will you ever learn?" Doug yells. "When will you get out of your own way? For God's sake, Gerette, you have been in *the work* for almost ten years!"

All I can muster is stunned silence.

"What the hell were you doing, asking Sandy about her 'frozen land'? That is only for her work with me. It's too deep to discuss with you. For crying out loud, you should know better. Opening this up in the wrong context could send her over the edge! You have to follow the rules. And do your homework!"

For a fleeting moment, I think, *I am following the rules.* But I stay quiet, because I know Doug is right. I'd learned about the part of me that pushes the rules, and I knew it as a form of "arrogance." I have a lot of pathological Jupiter in my chart, and I believe it is my greatest weakness.

In my mind's eye, I see Sandy and hear her telling me, "I'm not speaking from my wound, which is my homework. I'm sitting on the fence, ambivalent. This is a bad, bad place for me. I need help getting to the meat." She was quiet for a long time. I knew about her wound and how it was a place of power for her. I put my pen down, my heart full and waiting. Finally, she said, "There is a splinter in my head, it feels like I'm going crazy. I'm stuck in the frozen land."

This was the first time I'd heard about "the frozen land," and . . . *oh, right . . . this is where I must have gone wrong*. I must have asked her about it in an arrogant way. Shit. This is my learning edge . . . but wait . . . Doug had encouraged me to clarify, bring questions to him.

I'm confused.

Doug is still ranting. "All I ask is for you to do your homework. That's all. Then everything else will follow. His Love. Your success. It will all come, if you would only do your damn homework and stop trying to be Miss Know-It-All!" Now *I'm* in a frozen land.

"Do you get it?" he asks.

"Uhh . . . Yes. I think I do."

From the inside, Doug's tirade feels normal, and I cope in the only way I knew how: I leave. It is not safe to stay. My body stays right in front of him, but I press my core self into the shadows in a corner of the room and become very quiet, very still.

I am aware he is yelling; I've heard this before. Reality itself warps, aligning with Doug's words. I am at fault. I can't see that I am being condemned for doing exactly what he's told me to do: to ask questions.

I allow his authority to usurp my own. I forget the gentleness I'd felt with Sandy. I forget the compassion I'd felt for her, the caring that rose like cream to the surface of our sharing. I forget the questions I was burning to ask Doug, for his insight, so I can better understand what worked and what I'd missed, how I could do better. It is all gone, while I hover on the edge of darkness, dissociated.

He sighs, exasperated. "What's your dream?" A sliver of me returns to leaf through my journal, and I read:

> *I'm in the large two-story apartment of my old boyfriend,*
> *Ron. He is glad to see me and welcomes me in. I'm happy*
> *to see him and curious about his life now. He putters*
> *around his apartment. I ask if I should leave.*
>
> *"Please stay," he says, "but I have an appointment at*
> *two p.m." It's morning, so I stay. We chat while he does*
> *stuff. I feel awkward, but stay.*

Doug is excited about this dream, and tells me that it perfectly reveals where I am screwing up in Mentoring Group. "There you are, in the Animus's apartment, sneaking around, not really in relationship with him. This is exactly what you did with Sandy, not really being in true relationship with her."

Starting to see Doug's point, I ask if maybe I felt uncomfortable because Ron was not actively acknowledging me.

"You are always needing to be acknowledged, like in your shenanigans with Frank! You always want brownie points for being a good girl, for doing the right thing," Doug spits. "It's sickening. So childlike, when you could be actively in relationship with the Animus."

My homework from this dream is to be in the Animus's house, sneaking around, thinking I don't belong to him, and to be aware of how this pathology comes out in CTL, especially in the mentoring program. I am back to Phase One-style homework. I leave this session as I've left all sessions: determined to do better—and grateful I'd rejoined CTL.

Back in the fold, I share an email with CTL:

November 11, 2005

Thank you, Doug, for helping me to see how this dream reveals my sneaky, hiding pathology and how it is contaminating *the work*. I see how, in my mentoring sessions with all my mentees, I sneak around, try to be perfect, try to ask the right questions, desperately needing them to affirm me—because I do not have the connection with the man in order to live in my own skin. I see it. I am determined to keep seeing it and outing it until He purges this sickness from me. Although it pains me to see this disgusting insincerity, it's also freeing to 'out' it—I get what Doug means by 'outing the pathology' in a new way today. Outing means saying to the demon 'I see you and I see how you have tricked me, how you are holding me hostage.' And now I wait for His presence in my life to heal me. 'Please, Animus. Heal me.'

Now, from the outside, I reread my dream and feel touched by Ron's welcome, relishing the uncomfortable feeling of being with a man I once loved, grateful for the hours spent together.

The awkwardness I felt in the dream is and always has been familiar to me. To this day, I often feel awkward, unworthy, and imagine people don't want me around. I've struggled with this since I was a little kid, scared I would wet the bed at the slumber party. It's an insecurity that's woven into the essence of who I am. After several years of good therapy and a supportive writing practice, I have come to accept this part of me as one of my gifts.

Today—and in my dream, then—I don't shy from awkwardness. I

stay. Perhaps it's what helps me in my work as a cult educator. A client described how, before he started working with me, a licensed therapist literally threw her hands up in horror on hearing the details of the cult he was in.

No matter how dramatic or traumatic a cultic experience is, I will stay in the uncomfortable, non-judgmental space of acceptance as long as someone needs it. It's what I do. It's who I am.

An effectively controlling leader has an uncanny ability to hone in on the most vulnerable aspects of a person and twist reality, creating psychosis, at worst, and dependence, at best.

❧

The name of our training group kept changing, as its "purpose" came more and more into focus. From Mentoring Program to Basic Training, to Assistant Teachers in Training. We even had groups with endearing names, like Jenny's Jewels—for women who committed to a deep introspection of the feminine—and Doug's Dudes for the guys.

Each new manifestation of the process created an invitation to go deeper, to become more committed to supporting the growth of *the work* in the world. Eventually, the process gave birth to a training school for transformational learning. We all celebrated when we were approved to offer CEU's (Continuing Education Credits) for mental health staff. Our goal was to be fully accredited, so college students could choose to enroll in our classes and receive credit, but we never made it that far.

In CTL, we were continually being compared to each other, creating an undercurrent of competition. The lack of professional boundaries was invisible to me—I was already immersed in strengthening the "group-think." We were all unified by a common striving for the same goal, the same shiny carrot, always just barely out of reach. The banter of comparison wore me down, hollowed me out. I lost track of who I was, and I relied on my homework and Doug's coaching to anchor me.

From inside CTL, it didn't feel like the groups or the rules were constantly changing. It felt like progress. It felt like we were in this together, for the betterment of all of humanity. Because of this higher goal, it did not feel like we were slinging mud at each other, or that we were being trained to be fierce gladiators to entertain the one we revered.

But it was during the mentoring program that my mind snapped. Although my agency had been gradually eroding over the past ten years, this was the phase when the stakes were highest. I'd invested so much: moved my family, nearly lost my marriage, became an entrepreneur. I needed, really needed, *the work* to work.

I clung to a small patch of mind terrain around my business, my kids, and my husband, who thankfully was also in *the work*. I remained functional. I swept the floor after dinner and reminded the kids to do their homework, physically there in the kitchen but believing what was most important was my *own* homework. I hovered on the edge of my own psychological universe, which was becoming smaller and smaller, while believing I was growing, spiritually. This is when my mind slipped off the edge and fell asleep.

PART THREE

ASLEEP

"Through me is the way into the woeful city,
Through me is the way into eternal woe,
Through me is the way among the Lost People."
– From Dante's *Inferno* in *The Divine Comedy,*
translation by Charles Eliot Norton[9]

"Your body can't switch off tired. People fall asleep behind
the wheel all the time."
– Shanola Hampton[10]

Strangled

BRAD FOLLOWS CLOSE BEHIND ME, from the upper lean-to down to The Farm. My steps are hesitant, my heart heavy, and my ego humbled yet also oddly pleased with itself. In my last session, just before the retreat, Doug told me, "I'll only push hard if I feel you're ready for a breakthrough." I heartily agreed, praying this would be the retreat where my stubborn pathology would finally be broken.

To be assigned a watchdog partner during meals and between sessions was a special status. On one hand, it meant you need help, but on the other, that you were worthy of it. I'm ready for the challenge. Brad is the perfect person for the job—his six-foot-four football-player's stature makes him a powerful presence for his assignment: to strangle me when I speak from my pathology.

Doug had him practice. "Just put your hands around her neck. You don't have to use pressure. Your hands will be enough."

I contemplate this during the walk through the field, gazing across the valley to the wide spread of mountains beyond. Willy, my preferred group leader, is walking with Brad. I trust he will be there to clarify when Brad is unsure whether I'm speaking from my pathology. Willy knows me best, second only to Doug. My group members chat amicably as we walk together, but I picture myself a hawk, soaring on the thermals high above. Just outside The Farm's door, a small group has gathered.

"Were your dreams branched?" Pearl asks me as I approach. Branch Therapy, evolving from several dreams within the leadership circle, amplifies the dream's message when symbolic branches are placed between the parts of the dream where relationships are strongest. In my case, this time it's the absence of a limb that reveals the devastating isolation of my soul's experience. Pathology has the upper hand in my psyche this round.

"Yeah," I say. "It was fucking intense." I was unaware of Brad's presence for the brief moment it took to speak those words. Behind me, Willy nods to Brad, and two enormous hands encircle my throat. There is no pressure, but there doesn't need to be. I am silenced. Eyes closed, I try to ground myself, but confusion shoots like electrical short-circuits, coursing through my nervous system gone haywire. *Is it true that everything I say is bullshit pathology?*

I take a deep breath while Brad maintains his assigned position. I'm aware that Pearl is watching, and I sense her love, knowing she is rooting for me to get through this difficult piece of work, whatever it might be. I'm vaguely aware of the quiet when others notice Brad's hands around my throat, then slowly their chatter resumes.

In this setting, on this mountain, anything can happen. We are fierce about fighting the pathology that serves only to keep us from the emotional and spiritual freedom of living our lives according to God's plan.

For the moment, I am invisible, my anguish stretching to eternity while my psyche organizes itself around Doug's declaration that most of what I say cannot be trusted. I want to lean my head into Brad's sturdy body and let my broken self collapse into sobs of shame and confusion. I don't understand what this is all about. I allow myself to picture this release: Brad's arms would embrace my crumpled body. He would pick me up and carry me gently down the mountain, away from this burning confusion.

But I remain standing, accepting the medicine prescribed by my beloved teacher, and tell myself how grateful I am for this opportunity. Finally, the giant hands release, their work accomplished. We move inside and are swallowed by the savory smells of lunch, the bubbling chatter of laughter and clattering dishes.

If anyone felt uncomfortable about the strangling, they never told me. At least, not until after I left. The code of silence allowed such experiences to become a badge of honor for the victim and a dull wound for witnesses. We endured what our leader determined was best for us and repressed our instincts. To question the leader was to possibly become a target for ridicule or rejection. When Frank challenged Doug's preposterous statements, he was awarded the nickname Patho-trickster. In a seemingly playful, almost loving tone, Doug would warn Frank's retreat leader to "Watch out for Patho-trickster."

Several close friends now express regret for not standing up for me and others who were Doug's favorite targets. But, for them to defend us would have jeopardized their own inner work. Challenging Doug could have potentially undermined *their* process, or made them his next target. It was safer to stay quiet.

Sitting at the table with my group, I make it through the meal, not daring to venture away or speak with Frank, who is in a different group. I stay close to their comforting presence—they alone bore witness to my soul work in the upper lean-to. I'm grateful for their respectful dialog and loving glances as my silence grows.

Suddenly, Rob is at my side to check in about my Tech Team duties, setting up for the big group work. Willy raises his hand, stilling Brad's questioning impulse. There's no need to strangle me now—this is my CTL job. It is both a privilege and requirement to have a job at retreats.

Relieved to be able to talk, I quietly ask if John has returned the cables and mic to the tub by the speakers, and if the batteries for the lavaliers are fully charged. I feel a flash of gratitude. Maybe this strangling business is already helping me to be more focused and productive where it matters most—in my CTL work.

I make it through the afternoon and evening with only one additional strangling.

Later that evening, Frank and I finally connect after a full day in our respective small groups. Walking down to our sleeping shelter, arms wrapped around each other, I tell him about my Branch Work from earlier in the day, and Doug's intervention. Frank is very quiet. This silence makes me uncomfortable. I tell him, "I don't want to talk about it." The silence that stretches between us is a collision between longing to speak honestly and our trained discipline to protect CTL and Doug, above all else.

For Frank to speak against Doug on my behalf would have opened a wrath of accusation and ridicule. By this time, Doug has made it abundantly clear to CTL members that Frank cannot be trusted— hence his nickname, Patho-trickster. Frank has been identified by Doug as someone with the potential to be an excellent analyst, but who also could lure others into a dark, doubting rabbit hole. Frank and I both know silence is the safest way forward. That silence, compounded by thousands of other silences, supported a false narrative about both of us.

I couldn't afford to hear Frank speak, or my entire reason for being—twelve years of devotion and studies—would begin to unravel.

Journalist Benedict Carey writes "[. . .] social mores often work to shrink the space in which a conspiracy of silence can be broken: not at work, not out here in public, not around the dinner table, not here. It takes an outside crisis to break the denial."[11]

In CTL, for me, that crisis wouldn't come for another five years. Until then, I was unaware of being complicit in perpetuating Doug's condemning and false narrative about my husband and me. Today, I am awed by our resilience.

There are a few other times that weekend when Brad is prompted into action by my blasphemous talking. Each time, silence and confusion swirl as I wonder what pathology has snuck into what I've said, but I also trust that Willy is communicating with Doug about my progress, and I try not to worry about it.

In my first session after the retreat, I confess to Doug that I do not fully understand this intervention.

"It's a huge blind spot for you," Doug explains patiently. "You do it all the time—in your marriage, in your business. Always thinking you have the best idea, but never pausing to check in with *Him*."

Over time, I understand the importance Doug places on his intervention. I accept that my pathology is very tricky and that I need Doug's help to be able to see it. I accept that my arrogance wants to dominate everything I say. I see that Doug chose a dramatic intervention to help shake me from the bondage of this insidious, destructive inner beast that is determined to keep me from God's grace.

At every subsequent retreat, I am expected to describe Brad strangling me to the members in each retreat group, as an introduction to, and example of, my stubborn pathology and how I needed something dramatic to snap me out of its grip.

At every retreat that followed, for the next five years, Doug took delight in this experience. When he'd arrived at our lean-to to work my dreams, he'd ask the group, "Did she tell you about how we had to have Brad strangle her to get her to stop blowing smoke up her ass when she talked?"

He'd go on. "We had to! It was the only way to get her to stop!" And he would smile, shake his head, and look at me, beaming humor and love, which I tried to take in. Then he'd turn to Willy and ask, "Is it working? Do we need to get Brad back up here, or is she getting any better?"

Willy, an optimist like me, would answer, "I think so, Doug. I really think Gerette is staying in her work. Ya' know, she will get taken out here and there, especially with Frank, but by and large, she's doing really good work."

Then Doug would stretch out his hand like a gloved surgeon and Willy would hand him a piece of paper with my latest dreams neatly printed, my current homework succinctly stated in the header. And we'd begin the next round.

For years, I wrote confessional emails to the CTL registry, detailing my transgressions:

> I'm sorry I spoke out of line at Tuesday's meeting. My pathology often runs amuck when I speak, and is yet another example of how I can't be trusted. I am grateful for my uplink, who has my back on this issue.

The constantly changing "uplinks" were CTL members whom Doug promoted for their supposed ability to recognize pathology. In this hierarchal system, they needed only point a questioning finger at anything I said or did, and I'd know my pathology was lurking and would shut up or stop. Everything was reported to Doug. Each of these confessions was followed by some reference, articulated or not, about the strangling.

"The demand that one confesses to crimes one has not committed, to sinfulness that is artificially induced, in the name of a cure that is arbitrarily imposed [. . .]" is how Robert Jay Lifton speaks of "totalist confession."

From communist China to the Center for Transformational Learning, Robert Jay Lifton's research lifted the veil from my mind, once I got out. The totalist confession is one of the "eight deadly sins" that he identified through his research and experience with Korean prisoners of war and citizens of communist China in the 1950s.

Up in that lean-to, on the first day of my strangling, I submitted to Doug's artificially induced determination that I was possessed with a die-hard pathology that made me behave and speak like an idiot. I confessed to this sin hundreds of times thereafter, as I described my cure of strangulation, each time believing it a little more. After this experience, the only way I knew for sure if my words and decisions were "coming from the right place" was through Doug's affirmation.

My psyche was torn in two—a functioning, thoughtful, striving person who was a mother, wife, and business owner on the one hand; on the other, a dissociated woman bound by mind control, living in survival mode.

At each retreat following my strangling, there was a particular smile on Doug's face when he talked about this intervention. That smile would later haunt me. He'd tilt his head slightly, one side of his mouth curled up, the other lowered in friendly amusement. Back then, I believed it was the look of a man who loved me unconditionally and was fighting for my soul. Today, I recognize a snarl when I see one.

Bankrupt

"I DON'T KNOW HOW YOU lasted as long as you did." Mr. Chekowski's sad expression seems sincere, even though he will profit from our untenable situation. "I think we'll be able to save your home. And we can definitely keep this a personal bankruptcy. The business won't be affected."

Frank and I dare to glance into each other's eyes as shame, hope, and despair crash over us, with hope rising to the top for once. I want to reach out for Frank's hand, but let myself be content with our quivering knees touching as we face Mr. Chekowski across the enormous desk, which is nearly hidden under stacks of papers.

I scan my mind for my homework when Frank asks a question, but find myself trying not to cry instead. There are two storylines that led us to Mr. Chekowski's office. One is true, but I don't believe it.

In a couples session, Doug guides Frank and me through a long-standing conflict. Months earlier, I'd brought up the couch. I've been wanting to replace the uncomfortable futon couch for two years, to

100

make our living room feel more welcoming, a place for us and the kids to hang out. Doug asks us about it.

"The futon is fine and we don't have the money for a new couch right now," Frank says in his not-this-again voice. Doug doesn't know it, but Frank coined the term *Douganomics* for Doug's signature approach to finances. Even before Doug speaks, Frank says, "I think it's irresponsible to have such hubris around money. Things are tight for us, and I don't want debt."

Doug laughs him off. "For crying out loud, Frank, loosen up!" he chides. "There is nothing wrong with using your credit card. Buy a new couch for your wife!" Doug looks at me with compassion.

After a long silence, I realize that I'm ready to tell Frank about the recent business sessions. I'd scheduled four weekly sessions with Doug and Marie after she and I had a conflict, determined to not let pathology destroy our working relationship and the business. Through this intensive, we were able to unearth my deepest soul wound, and I'd not yet been able to share it with anyone, including Frank. With Doug's help, I'm now able to describe the hopeless place within me.

"It is a dark, desolate land in my soul that seems to have occurred in a past life, where I lost faith in God and went into survival mode." I start quietly and gain confidence when I see Doug nod. Frank and I had attended the class together when Doug first started teaching about past-life trauma. It was a riveting lesson. I force myself to continue.

"For me, the problem is less about the desolation and more about how I responded to it. Through my dreams and all we've been learning about past-life trauma"—I look at Doug and feel strengthened to continue—"I see that I developed terrible habits during that time. I was in survival mode, without God's love—anxious and defensive— and I learned to manipulate others to get what I needed. *I learned to lie and cheat.* This became my modus operandi." Feeling Doug's support, I continue, "Defensiveness and manipulation became ingrained soul habits during that past life; and now, through the transformational learning process, I can see how they are surfacing every day at work. It is so intense to see it."

I am shaking and need to take a break. Frank is quiet, his eyes soft when they meet mine. I take a few deep breaths. Doug looks at me with compassion and says quietly, "It's great to see you this clear and vulnerable. Are you ready to share your homework?"

I take a deep breath and look out the window while I mentally ground myself with my homework.

Doug announced every month, in his advanced teacher training class, "There will be more people wanting to do this work than we have analysts to handle them!"

Jenny regularly posted the new arrivals on the email registry. "Two new people today!" The subject line would read. "Another new one!" "Caught another one!"

I felt an electrical charge each time I'd read such announcements. Doug always said, "*Shine a light in the dark, and people will come.*"

Once smitten by the emperor, agreeing with the preposterous became a reflexive habit. In the process of becoming his devotee, discernment disappeared. The emperor's status demanded the trust of his minions, and groupthink unified them.

"Indeed, these are the finest clothes I have ever seen!" Silence strengthened with each new believer. Until one brave, or innocent, or simply honest person dared blurt out, "Either I am blind, or you are naked!"

I was aligned with Doug, admiring the finely woven cloth and his fancy designs. But, by doing so, I, too, was naked.

Letting out a long sigh, I'm ready to go on with our couples session. "Yes, there's more. Frank—I have to tell you that it's *only* through the teamwork of both Marie and Doug bringing examples to my attention that this core-trauma wound is finally being exposed. There are lots of examples with my staff and customers. Like . . . oh, jeez . . . I can't think of an example right now, but like, you know—how I was lying about money and manipulating what was really going on in the business."

I pause, look straight at Frank, and continue. "My inner work now is to recognize when I am triggered into that survival mode, and to really notice what I'm doing. Once I see my behavior clearly, then I have to do two things: bring compassion to myself, acknowledging this as a past-life trauma reaction; and then STOP DOING IT!" I giggle and smile with Doug and Frank. Levity, thank goodness. I finish by saying, "I am finally understanding that my work as a business owner is really about healing my soul."

Doug interjects here: "And since you are learning to relate in a truly honest, authentic way, this will spill over into your marriage, too. That's the power of healing past-life trauma—all aspects of life are healed. It's healing the core wound."

Putting a hand on each of his thighs, as if ready to leap from his chair, Doug looks at each of us with a smile and says, "This was a breakthrough couples session. Great work, guys."

"Things are really tense at the office right now," Frank says at the end of a long week soon after that session. "There will likely be a bunch of lay-offs."

Later that same week, we shop for and buy a couch on credit, even though it makes Frank nervous. We sign up for CTL classes and retreats, knowing we can use Doug's payment plan if we can't pay for them right away. For the first time in our relationship, we accrue credit card debt that we can't pay off every month.

Then Frank loses his job.

But I am relieved. Frank pitches in to help with my business. Having expanded to include auto detailing and carpet cleaning, I am in way over my head. I'm determined, though. Now, we can turn the corner into a profitable business where God's love will call the shots.

I don't know what it means to "look at the bottom line," or "review projections," or even how to create a budget. But Frank has not yet found a new job. In the midst of the recession, there is nothing out there for him to apply for. Besides, it seems unnecessary. And I'm trying to break free from fear-based thinking.

Months stretch into more than a year, but I don't notice. Reality for me is sound bites from one session to the next class, to the next retreat or CTL email. When I finally tell Doug that our accountant recommends we see a bankruptcy lawyer, he cheers. "Alleluia! It's about time you saw the light. Now maybe I won't have to listen to you complain about money so much!"

When I burst into tears, he softens. "There is no shame in it, Gerette. I hope you can find peace. People file for all kinds of reasons. And now, you two can have a clean slate. I hope you will use it to open your hearts to *the work* in a new way."

We've been back in Timberland for over three years now, and it *is* thrilling to participate in CTL's growth. Books are being published about our signature transformational learning approach. People from all over the world are finding us through our website. Doug is being interviewed on national stations, and we're offering workshops and retreats all over North America, and beyond.

Doug is right. With so much abundance and promise, I don't need to stress too much over money.

Even so, I complain in one of my sessions. "I don't know, Doug. We're both working really hard, but we just can't seem to keep our heads above water."

"That's your problem—trying to keep your heads above water! Let go and ride the rapids, let the water take you down. That's where you will meet Him." Doug reminds me about my many river dreams. "God doesn't want you to worry about money," he goes on. "Spend what you have. No need to hide away money for a rainy day—that's what squirrels do."

This is not my first experience with bankruptcy. A year before my parents divorced, they filed, too. We lost the farm; the cows were sold off at auction. I couldn't watch out the window when the large trailer filled with our girls rattled away down the farm road. It was weeks before I could enter the empty barn. The soul of the farm left with the cows.

I still woke at dawn, out of habit, and wondered who was milking them. We kids also scattered with the divorce. Clara and I moved away with Dad. Raymond and Kat moved out, beginning their own adult lives. My other three sisters stayed on with Mom. Bankruptcy, loss, and divorce forge an indelible link in my tender teenage heart.

No wonder I worry that Frank and I won't make it. I keep scanning for fault lines in our marriage, and so far, so good. The vanilla episode was behind us. But growing debt, Frank's sudden layoff, and the other storyline, one we won't be able to understand until years later, fueled our downward spiral.

Although finances at home are in ruins, the cleaning business is solvent. Marie is paid well for her work as office manager, all the employees are paid, and Kim Hanlon (who I'd bought the cleaning company from) receives her five hundred dollars a week. I get whatever is left, which varies from week to week.

I can feel the potential in this business and trust my time will come.

But one thing concerns me. As much as I love and trust Marie, there is growing tension in our working relationship, which prompts me to schedule extra sessions with Doug to help get us back on track.

A couple of months before we filed for bankruptcy, I had a private session with Doug immediately after discovering the previous week's billing had not been completed, putting us in a precarious position for making payroll.

In a rare emotional moment, I vented to Doug: "Sometimes it feels like Marie checks out when I need her to show up the most! I am so frustrated!"

I was not prepared for Doug's response.

"Marie may never change. She is just so damaged."

I was accustomed to suppressing my responses to Doug's often dramatic statements. But this one felt like a knife entering the soft flesh of my belly. While the words "she is just so damaged" echoed in my mind, Doug was still talking.

"It doesn't seem like the Animus is interested in your business anymore."

Doug's words were a death sentence that I do not accept. I work harder than ever, but also try to be smarter, more discerning about decisions I make with my staff. I cannot articulate to anyone—not Frank, not even Doug—how much Doug's two statements disturb me. I suppress them.

And before long, Marie gives her notice, Frank is laid off, and we spiral out of control, ending up in Mr. Chekowski's office.

Captured Woman

MARIE'S DEPARTURE PROMPTS A RESTRUCTURING. Finances are eased somewhat without her salary, I renegotiate the terms for paying Kim, and I'm up for the challenge of developing new systems to better serve me, my employees, and my customers. Thankfully, Amy, a longterm and stellar employee, has eagerly stepped into the manager position, bringing new and needed efficiencies. But, no matter how organized I am, there seems to be no end to the work.

I arrive early to savor a quiet office moment before the crew starts arriving. I check phone messages and am surprised to hear Mr. Schroeder, a steady customer, terminating his biweekly cleaning service in a curt message left at 2 a.m. I'm unsettled to lose a customer and wonder about his reasons. Then the phone rings.

"I need you to return to the house as soon as possible." The woman's voice has an edge to it, and I struggle to absorb what she tells me: *she* owns the house we'd been cleaning, not Mr. Schroeder. It hadn't occurred to me that he might be renting. "It's being emptied out now.

I'd like your company to do a thorough deep clean." The tension in her voice is palpable. What's really going on here?

"I'm surprised by how suddenly he is leaving the house," I pry.

"Well"—she pauses—"I will tell you in confidence"—pause again—"I've initiated an investigation into Mr. Schroeder, because I have evidence he was holding a woman there against her will."

My breath catches.

A woman held captive.

The very first time I take the long, darkly wooded driveway to Mr. Schroeder's house, I dismiss a flutter of fear. I am poised but unnerved while giving him an estimate for cleaning his capacious home. Everything is tidy, but I notice mildew in the bathroom, fur-like dust on the exposed beams of the cathedral ceilings, and the tile and pine floors need a good washing.

I write down his instructions about Christine, the woman living in the basement apartment who must be a caretaker of sorts. "Christine will be your primary contact, because I am often working overseas." Mr. Schroeder has an international marketing business.

But when he mentions a second woman on the first floor, my mind prickles. "Under no circumstances will you clean her bedroom. She is sick, and takes care of it herself."

But . . . if she's sick, isn't it more *important that we clean for her?* I don't ask. His brusque manner makes it clear there's no time for such indulgence. Besides, I've trained myself to not question others, to override my own sense of right and wrong, because, as Doug tells me, "You are finally learning how contrary you are! Almost everything you do and think is the exact opposite of what God wants for you."

When I glance at the closed door to the woman's bedroom, I feel uneasy but push it aside, finish my notes, and tell Schroeder I will email an estimate within forty-eight hours.

I step into the fresh, quiet air, relieved to be back outdoors. As I walk to my car, a little brown bird flits in the trees beside me. It hops from one branch to another, as if it has something to tell me. I gaze into the towering trees and filtered light, and remember my current homework: Jump into the crevasse, and STAY with The Man. I close my eyes and try to visualize the dreams I brought to Doug in yesterday's session, recalling his urgent interpretation of the two dreams spliced together.

"This is it, Gerette! It's time for you to die to self." Doug was excited. "Instead of clinging to safety, you need to jump into the crevasse—and STAY with The Man. Let *Him* lead you."

I force myself to imagine the moment I experienced in my session, and feel again the fear of falling through darkness, then being greeted by a man who wore a shiny belt buckle. My eyes flash open as I remember Doug's admonishing voice as I left the session: "And don't do anything stupid—like project your fear and sabotage your business!"

My mind races: Am I projecting my fear onto the woman who lives on the main floor? Did I come off as a pompous ass to Schroeder? He seems like a great client. I hope I haven't blown it already.

The bird has disappeared. I hop in the car and check my phone, where I find a text from Amy with an update on the team up north.

Damn. No cell service here. I suddenly feel claustrophobic and tear down the driveway, eager to get back into the open. Before pulling onto Route 106, I prompt myself again to "jump into the crevasse" in response to Doug's urgent plea. "You need to do your homework twenty times an hour—to break your stubborn will—so you can die to the divine that is waiting for you."

I know Doug's voice in my head better than my own. As I pass the open fields of Sunny Dale Farm, I take a deep breath and coach myself calm. If it had not been for Doug and *the work*, I would never be where I am now. I love what I'm doing. I feel the presence of the Animus, and take a long swig of water.

Schroeder accepts my estimate for both an initial deep clean and our ongoing biweekly cleaning service. I return to his house a dozen times over the following year to oversee my employees and to fill in when someone calls in sick. Our instructions clearly indicate that no one is to enter the first-floor bedroom, and no one ever does.

When they hear that Schroeder's cancelled his service, the staff start talking.

"I was always creeped out in that house."

"I heard the woman crying once. I felt so awful."

"He kept a freakin' Glock under his pillow."

"And a shotgun under the bed, too!"

"He *always* wore a gun. I was always relieved when he wasn't there."

"That Christine who lived in the basement was *weird*. She was like a scared, caged dog."

During the last cleaning of the house, the one paid for by the real owner, Amy and I entered the first-floor bedroom, clutching each other's arm. The room was completely empty. We opened the closet and saw fresh holes in the wall where *something* had been removed. As we exited the room, Amy pointed to the door knob, which locked only from the outside. We can't get out of that room fast enough.

The next week, I have a session with Doug and tell him how disturbing it is for me to consider the allegations against Mr. Schroeder. Doug thinks I'm going off into unnecessary tangents and asks for a dream, saying, "When in doubt, let the dream correct us."

> *I'm a teenager, alone, and I enter an abandoned house.*
> *I see the torso of a deer on the kitchen floor. I feel scared*
> *and go further into the house. I look down the basement*

110

*stairs, and there, at the bottom, is the rest of the deer—
the head, the legs.*

*I am scared, filled with pain—the deer is me. A teenage
boy enters the house, and now I'm scared in a different
way. I think he is the one who killed the deer. He comes in
close behind me and I elbow him, hard, right in the face.*

*I'm not sure if I actually elbow him or just imagine
doing it.*

Doug becomes animated, responding to this dream. He tells me
how it confirms his suspicions that I am overreacting to the story
about Mr. Schroeder and the captive woman. He compares it to the
way I overreacted to the boy who came up behind me in my dream,
smashing him in the face.

"The boy is the real you, Gerette—and you smash his face! This is
how you hurt yourself and hurt others. You think the boy killed the
deer, but that happened long ago. That's the trauma you need to stay
with, not attacking the boy in you, the one that comes to help you."
Doug sighs into a long silence, then looks straight at me and says,
"You can never get further from yourself than when you want to kill
the very thing that is most innocent."

It's my turn for silence as I write in my journal in bold letters:

"I CAN NEVER GET FURTHER FROM MYSELF THAN
WHEN I WANT TO KILL THE VERY THING THAT IS
INNOCENT IN ME."

When patriarchy is ingrained in a culture—like ours—the inherent
power of the feminine becomes a silent enemy. The balance of power
in American culture sways undeniably in favor of men. Encoded into
the DNA of every controlling group are unconscious, implicit biases
that define the organization through multilayered webs of subtly

coercive kinetics.

Was femininity itself a threat in Doug's psyche, being broadcast throughout all of CTL? Were Doug's male heroes—his obsession with the Animus—embedding spiritual misogyny?

Doug goes on. "When you open your mouth to blab, blab, blab, you are avoiding the pain and fear. When you talk that way, you are attacking the boy—and others—all the while thinking that you are a good person and believing you have something good to say, appearing smart, choosing your words carefully, no spontaneity—you are always, always in control!"

I am furiously writing while Doug speaks. I can tell this is a blind spot for me, and I really want to get through this. I want to get it right. Doug keeps talking. He's in lecture mode now, which always feels like he is "channeling" the Animus.

"Smashing the boy in the face is revealing how much hate is in you. You hate the death of the deer. You need to look into the eyes of the devil—and the devil is what you have become. You really need to see this. It is so strong, a self-fulfilling cycle. If you don't see it, the more power it has over you—it will never end."

He pauses again, looking out the window before going on. "You are always talking, blowing smoke up your ass and everyone else's ass. You are so invested in being in control. It's never just a simple conversation with you. You are *always* manipulating. You need to see this, to keep it clear, to see what you do and say. To be the boy is to be abused by someone. In the past, maybe a past life, who knows, you were abused, and now this has turned into you abusing your own innocence. It's the same thing as what you do in your business—lying and manipulating. You attack the innocence in others, too! Like your customer, this Schroeder guy. You have *no* idea what is going on in his house, *and it's none of your business!*"

My hand starts to cramp from taking notes. But he's not done.

"You've got to be aware of this energy when you speak to others. *This* is what's under your damn pride and under that sappy sentimentality you have. Can't you see it? Manipulation masks the rage. And the rage is what really runs the show. You have so much rage in you! You smash the boy in the face. You need to accept that this hate lives in you, and wait for the next dream. Pride masks the abuse." He pauses and I look up at him. I can tell he is not done yet. My pen is ready.

"The ass kisser in you is so resistant. It is astonishing how resistant you are to *the work*. It is clear you're not working hard enough. You do your work in spurts, which is not enough!" Doug sighs. "I'm growing weary of your game of not fighting your own pathology. I'm not getting the return, the cooperation from you. I'm trying too hard to help you." He stands, saying, "*I'm* the one climbing up the mountain for you, and I can't do this anymore!"

Then he looks at me, exasperated. "It takes more than what you have been doing to break your stubborn pathology! You're holding onto your shit too much. You have to REALLY COMMITT TO THE ASSIGNMENT!!" Then he sighs and ends his address, saying, "I'm running out of love . . ."

There's a long silence as I finish my notes. I am meek. "What's my homework?"

"What do you think it should be?" He taunts me.

"Well, something about not talking the way I usually do."

"Right! Maybe you are finally getting it. 'DO NOT TALK'—and when you do, because we know you will, notice how you're smashing the boy in the face."

I write down my homework:

DO NOT TALK! And when I do . . . know that I'm smashing the boy in the face.

When I got out of CTL and began my quest to understand how I could've let it get so bad, I was shocked to reread my journals and listen to recorded sessions from this time period. My journals and recordings hold the link between the fabricated narrative that damned me to dependence on Doug, and who I really am. Doug used a cursory understanding of trauma, layered with a juicy past-life cosmology, and taught me to excavate for something that did not exist. Now that I *am* talking, I have to wonder why Doug was so determined to silence me. What lies and manipulations needed to come out into the light?

Later that day, I text Doug with a question about Media Committee. After a couple exchanges around logistics, I thank him for the day's session, saying how helpful it was. He answers, uncharacteristically, with a quote from the Bible:

"He that walks in darkness knows not where he goes."

I'm touched to receive this after-hours blessing from Doug, and look up the whole passage of John 12:35:

"Yet a little while is the light with ye. Walk while ye have the light, lest the darkness come upon you: for he that walketh in the darkness knows not wither he goeth. While ye have light, believe in the light, that ye may become the sons of light."[12]

I contemplate this and feel grateful to have Doug to help me discern the light from the dark. I put aside my worries about Mr. Schroeder and whatever may or may not have occurred in that house.

Through dreams, astrology, trauma work, past life experience, and an elaborate conceptual framework, *the work* became for me what Lifton calls a "sacred science," which held out an "ultimate moral vision for the ordering of human existence." In this way, I fell into line, as have the millions of people influenced by Communist China's brainwashing techniques, not to mention untold numbers of cultic groups across the globe.

The charges against Mr. Schroeder were dropped, but when I step back and look at the whole picture, I sense him guilty. I also recognize the uneasy parallels between myself and the woman in the first-floor bedroom.

I can identify the dissociated state I was in after Doug's condemning interpretation of my dream and his response to the events that unfolded in that house. I wonder how he could hear my description of the situation and not be alarmed enough to at least encourage me to report what I knew. Doug's propensity to side with the masculine set me up to deny my feminine instinct.

What factors supported me—an intelligent, moral woman—to keep my head down and scrub toilets when I sensed something was off? Years of grooming in the spiritual superiority of men had led me to defer to men in general. I deferred to Doug's interpretation of my dreams in every biweekly session with him, for over eighteen years. I deferred to the group leaders who I trusted most, all men. So, naturally, in interactions with this customer—a man—I deferred to his requests and suppressed my discomfort. As long as I was a member of CTL, whenever I interacted with men and money, I deferred.

Shortly after breaking away from CTL, a dear friend who I'd nearly lost taught me one of her life mottos, which I adopted: If it sounds right, but it doesn't feel right, it's not right.

If it sounds right, but it doesn't feel right, it's NOT right.

You can never get further from yourself than when you want to kill the very thing that is most innocent. A woman can never get further from herself than when she defers her feminine knowing to a teacher who is blinded by a patriarchy that condemns the very essence of being female.

The unseen woman in Schroeder's house and I lived very different realities, but we shared some common, sinister threads. She was held physically against her will; I went about my life as a "free" woman, but my mind and soul were not my own.

How could I be accountable, if I did not have full access to my own thoughts and instincts? My instincts were trapped in an energetic reversal: what I should fear, I ignored. And I focused my time and life energy on issues that were fundamentally nonsensical: "Jump into the crevasse and stay with the man with the shiny belt buckle."

I sense now, that my dream about the broken deer and the teenage boy possessed a powerful message for me, from me. In that scathing session with Doug, he ignored the fact that I was a teenager in the dream. As a farm girl, I was often around the severed body parts of animals. My brother hunted deer. We slaughtered sheep, cows, and chickens on a regular basis. I am not squeamish.

❧

A freshly slaughtered lamb hangs in the pole barn. The butcher sharpens, then draws his knife from throat to groin, and the animal's inside is revealed. I am in awe.

For a brief eternity, I take in the glistening pink, perfectly ordered universe, organs of symmetry and asymmetry. A symphony of the spheres. This moment of divinity—before the butcher's next move— remains one of the most visceral moments of beauty in my life—right up there with giving birth.

❧

I didn't run from the sight of the deer's body in my dream. I continued into the house to see the truth, the disturbing reality of body severed from head and legs. I know this deer was me—*my head and legs are not someone's trophy!*

I'm flooded with injustice when the boy comes too close. I don't know if this boy has hacked my deer-self, or if it was someone else. I don't know if the boy intends to harm me. Either way, he's invading my space and I will not stay quiet about his transgression against this deer. I speak, with the instinct to give myself room to be who I am. I speak with my elbow.

Was this dream a response to the knowledge of my proximity to the captured woman? A bid to rouse my conscience to take action against Mr. Schroeder? Was this dream an attempt to wake my teenage self into action, to shout down the injustice of how I was being dismembered through convoluted ideals I'd grown to believe were gospel?

In the patriarchal vacuum of Doug's ideology—and my blind adherence to it—there was no place for my feminine instinct to get a foothold, to sink into the earth of truth. In my pre-Doug state of mind, would I have found some way to learn more about the woman behind the door, instead of staying obedient and compliant at the request of a man? And, more importantly: what will I do differently, if ever in a similar situation?

These questions land uncomfortably in the pit of my post-cult stomach. They also make me feel more alive. My heart aches when I think of this unnamed woman and how close I'd been to her. Was she listening while I scrubbed the dark, cement-bodied floor tiles in the hallway, just outside her locked door?

"Who cares? You never even met her. It's none of your business." The voice in my head is familiar, but I can't place it. Then, I recognize its dismissive edge. In a surge of ire, I realize it is Doug's. In almost every session I had with him, when I spoke about something that was meaningful to me, he would mockingly ask, "Who cares?"

I rise now from my chair, gaze out my window, feel my feet on the ground, and say out loud, "I DO! I CARE!"

I care about the unnamed women who've been silenced. I care about reclaiming our voices. I care about speaking the truth when injustice has oppressed me or one of my sisters.

But Doug's campaign, condemning me to silence, shutting down my feminine instinct and confidence to be able to communicate honestly, waged on for several more years.

Mystical Marriage

AS THE SPARK BETWEEN JENNY and Doug grows from romance into marriage, the divine feminine emerges front and center in *the work*. Finally. I'm not alone in welcoming this change—it's a long-overdue correction. Jenny leads the way, sharing dream after dream about her girl-self, which emerges as she navigates a love relationship with the man who was once her analyst and teacher.

Suddenly many of us, men and women alike, have dreams about girls and women. These dreams bear new meaning, as Doug and Jenny have insights about the essential nature of "the girl" as an archetype. They begin teaching classes together about the boundless potential of living life in harmony with our inner girl-child.

"The archetypal girl feels *everything*," Jenny teaches in Living Dreams class. She tells us her dream about a girl, about six years old, holding her doll, which is on fire, flames engulfing much of the doll's soft body. "She is not separate from her doll. Her heart lives in her doll's heart, and she feels the pain of those flames, just as if she herself was on fire."

This period is a renaissance for *the work*, a flowering of forces arising from a fruitful balance of feminine and masculine. I feel more motivated to bring *the work* into the world, because I believe these enhancements will bear fruit in CTL's public image. Jenny's passion and grace balances Doug's rough edges, bringing credibility and wholeness to *the work*.

Although we have benefited from her skills with group facilitation for years, as the two of them become one in life partnership, *the work* takes on a whole new dimension. With the arrival of the feminine comes a sense of deepening around trauma work, including the groundbreaking "regressive dreaming."

Through a series of dreams Doug and Jenny share openly, a riveting past-life story builds, coinciding with a retreat at a castle in the Alsace region in Germany. Through their dreams and instructions from the divine, the couple plumb their emotional and spiritual depths to reveal that they were married in a past life, living as Christian mystics who inspired a devotional community. Together, they lived in transcendent harmony with God and the Earth during the twelfth century. Trauma was also woven into the tapestry of their previous life together. Their story becomes increasingly vivid— through the dreams they report having—in the months leading up to their nuptial vows.

They lived in a remote, mountainous village, until they were persecuted for heresy and witchcraft. When the medieval military set siege to their community, Doug was able to escape, only to be hanged later. Jenny remained with her people, who prayed and fasted while soldiers prepared her public execution. The people's devotion to God was so great, some of the devotees begged for their own beheading beside that of their beloved leader.

We in CTL believed that the emergence of the girl, the divine feminine, laid the foundation for us to reckon with the cognizant discord of past-life trauma. Naturally, dreams of past-life traumas became frequent within our community, and many of us found that we, too, were part of this devotional community that ended in devastation. Had we found each other here in the mountains of New York, the hunting territory of the Kanien'kehá:ka, to further the work we'd started back in the twelfth century?

What is belief, but an attitude? Liberty of belief is woven into our constitution, the ground we walk on, in the New World—freedom of religion. It's something we choose, whether true or false, real or fabricated.

I worked my fingers to the bone to attend the Alsace retreat in Germany, believing *this* was my moment in *the work*. I didn't know the phenomenon of "belief perseverance" then—the tendency to hold onto a belief even when it is not in one's best interest. I believed that *this* retreat, once and for all, would establish that I was worthy. In the unspoken recess of my mind I sensed, like a hunter nearing his prey, that once it was revealed that I, too, perished as spiritual kin in this past life, I would finally become an accepted and respected member of the "family," and would no longer need to grovel for acknowledgment. Belief does not require active introspection.

❧

One of my earliest little-girl memories is leaning my cheek and forehead into the cool, smooth glass of our car window as we travel north. When our family piled into the Buick station wagon for a rare summertime outing, window seats were coveted. No one wanted to be squished in the middle with all seven kids packed in the back and the way-back—which was a far-lesser second choice. Slowing for a gas station prompted a chorus. "I get the window seat next!" "I get the way-back!"

With my head pressed against the window, I sing to the trees, birds, and bushes we pass. Or were they passing us? I sing in greeting and in adulation. I smoosh myself to the window, my creation song merging me with the passing hills. I try to keep my voice quiet to avoid the inevitable swift elbow jab snapping me out of my reverie. "Would you shut up? You're driving me crazy."

I zip my mouth, but my forehead remains glued to the window, my gaze outward. The car door begins to melt, and the trees come nearer . . .

"You're doing it again!" my sister complains.

❧

I've kept up my monotonous singing into adulthood. After our farm went bankrupt and Mom and Dad divorced a year later, I learned to sing with the flute on the rickety porch of the home where Clara, Dad, and I lived for a month, before we settled into a refurbished schoolhouse on a dirt road, where I sang into the wind. Wide-open hay fields rolled in soft peaks and valleys, affording me places to hide from the road, and from the life I didn't want to leave behind. My dad thought I was hiding from myself, too. But he was wrong. Those walks were my salvation and solace. With my face pressed into the wind, I sang my gratitude for the Earth and her creatures. I sang as loud as I wanted. No one elbowed me to shut up.

When Dad discovered the nearby Mount Savior Monastery, a Benedictine hermitage that welcomed visitors on Sunday mornings, he brought Clara and me. We loved going there. The brothers' simple life, their harmonious chanting, their sheep and rolling pastures, all seemed to resonate at a similar pitch to my own. Through the winter we went on most, but not all, Sundays.

Dad and I would sometimes have conversations about the message offered in the service. I told him how much I appreciated the brothers' gentle relationship to Nature, how it resonated with my own. I even told my father how I sometimes experienced God in Nature. He seemed to understand.

When spring came, the wind called to me. I left my dad a note early one Sunday morning, "I'm going to 'church' in the fields today! Have a nice time at Mount Savior. Not sure what time I'll be back."

I set off soaring, a hawk riding a thermal. Returning home many hours later, I was flush with contentment, but was greeted with a dart.

"Finally back from your 'church' in the fields, I see," my father sneered on the word *church*. "How was your child's play?"

I was stunned and silenced. I'd believed my father saw and accepted me for who I was.

This did not change my loyalty to my father. I'd been in staunch support of him when we lost the farm, and through the divorce. I'd seen his spiteful vengeance lash out at my mother and hated it, but I did not turn away from him. I witnessed his reckless drunkenness, driving home with Clara and me at night, but I stayed. I listened to endless rants of bitterness toward our mom and toward politics, and my allegiance to him endured.

I retracted from him in horror at his behavior toward my sisters when Raymond died, but I did not abandon him. I remained until his deathbed, as one of two daughters who still spoke with him. The other four had pulled up their stakes and moved on.

Through my dedication to my father and the structures he endorsed and enforced, I remained a dutiful daughter. I loved my father. Still do. Although I stayed by him after he ridiculed my church, I would no longer be vulnerable enough to share my soul's depth. I saved that part of me for Doug—hoping against hope to heal this and other wounds from my father's darts.

❧

Jenny's elevation beside her husband heralds the feminine. My lifelong creed of reverence for Mother Earth is activated, inspiring ever-deepening commitment to *the work*. I join the executive committee, and after months of coaching, earn the privilege of becoming the official note taker. I am entrusted with the sensitive information of payment plans. As responsibilities up at The Farm and within CTL are growing, I fly to Germany, despite our shoestring, post-bankruptcy budget, hopeful for the new life the Alsace Retreat will open up for me.

The teachers are sitting on the front porch of the gasthaus. Ice cubes swirl in their drinks as they talk with ease and intimacy. Their laughter wafts toward me, musical notes of joy reaching my ears. I feign nonchalance when I pass by or dare to approach them. The wall that separates me from them is just as visceral here as it was back home. I refuse to reveal my sadness, lest I appear needy. I am too far along in *the work* for that.

On the last night of the retreat, I sleepwalk for the first and only time in my life. I wake up when my roommate is startled, because I've opened the balcony door.

She calls, "Gerette?!?"

Awake now, I notice my bare feet gripping the edge of the balcony. A breeze billows my nightgown, and I look down at the stone patio below. *Where was I going?*

❧

I am honored to participate in Doug and Jenny's wedding in the spring after the Alsace retreat, when more than two hundred people fill The Farm to capacity to witness the mystical marriage. The ceremony, officiated by Willy and Pearl, features a psychodramatic reenactment of Doug and Jenny's past-life story. Frank, wearing a black hood, plays the part of executioner. I am one of the devotees, offering up my own head beside Jenny's. We all perish, but rise again, victorious. We join together to rejoice in the union of our devoted leaders.

ॐ

A decade later, I muse about the singular burning question I'd brought to my first session with Doug, and a pattern of cultic coercion reveals itself to me. Sexuality, where we are at our most vulnerable *and* most potent, is controlled in one way or another in every cult I've met. In the heart of our most private selves, a leader or doctrine sneaks in, leaving bread crumbs, setting traps and smokescreens in our deepest, most intimate selves. I have no answers, only more questions simmering into a desire to delve more fully into these mysteries, with cognition intact and engaged.

The Chandelier

I STEP ONTO THE FIRST rung of the ladder and recall Doug's story about what happened when John replaced the siding on the north wall of the retreat center.

"He sets up the ladder, puts on his tool belt, climbs up the ladder, and at the very top, reaches for his hammer." Here Doug pauses, his right hand reaching for his imaginary hammer. He smiles, looking around the large circle of retreat participants, then walks over to John and places his hand gently on his shoulder. "But he couldn't find it. Turns out, he'd left his hammer on my back porch."

Groans and giggles twitter around the circle—Doug's house is an hour's drive from The Farm. Our collective gaze settles on John in loving humor. This was a classic John move, and we tease him for this and many other such mishaps.

Now, it's my turn to help out, and I hope there will be no stories worth telling afterward. John has set up three tiers of scaffolding for the chandelier-cleaning project I've been planning for months. Today is only the second time the chandelier has been cleaned since The Farm was built, almost a decade ago. The first time, it was done by Clear Sky Window, which cost a fortune. This time, I assure Doug I can take care of it for a fraction of the cost, as long as I have John's help with the scaffolding. I check my cleaning apron and bucket: cloths, glass cleaner, scrubby, squeegee, razor, whisk broom, extra cloths. John told me he was certain the scaffolding was safe.

Standing alone in this building I revere, I muse how much *the work* has deepened since Branch Therapy was added. It was a brilliant addition to dream enactment, brought about after a few teachers dreamt of trees with their branches all lit up. They were extraordinary dreams with many details, and Doug determined they were instructions from the Divine, prompting us to start using actual branches when enacting dreams: where there is an especially strong relationship between different parts or characters, the actors hold a branch between them. This simple addition is a surprisingly powerful tool in our visioning of the dream.

Years ago, I dreamt of fussing over a small child. In our reenactment, someone played the role of the child while I crooned over her, straightening her hair, cooing and generally fussing, as mothers often do. After a moment Willy, the group leader, had us hold a short branch between us. Once the branch was in my hands, I felt the connection more strongly.

In the same dream, however, I was scared of a man wearing a black coat. There was no branch between me and the man, who was certainly the Animus, in our role-play. In this dream enactment, I viscerally felt how I'd used fussing over the child to avoid my fear of, and turning toward, relationship with the Animus. Often, it is the lack of a branch that speaks most clearly. When Doug and Jenny started offering retreats and workshops in other places, we switched from using branches to yarn, for ease of transport.

I step onto the sturdy wooden plank of the first landing on the scaffold and remember what it was like in the early days, when my work was primarily about recognizing pathology and the various ways I turned my back on archetypal support.

In one memorable dream, I'd been obsessed with smoothing out wrinkles in a tablecloth while the Anima sang in another room. I remember holding the branch that linked me to the tablecloth. Yes, we also played the roles of inanimate objects in our dreams: airplanes, houses, tornados. We'd step into whatever the psyche delivered. This is part of the fun—and the mystery of the process. But when I heard the Anima sing and looked at the space between us with no branch, I was filled with longing to be with her. This longing was a breakthrough for me, supporting my striving to go deeper.

I take a breath and climb the second ladder. The second phase of *the work* is all about relationship—discovering we are not alone. As Doug teaches, Divine support is always available if we are open to it. I think of all my "wild cat" dreams: the cheetah streaking past me, wild kits playing, and a lion placing his massive paw on my head. I had so many dreams with lambs and teenagers, interpreted as bringing me back to the vitality of my younger self, still engaged in the world, before my ego took over and usurped my gentle connection with the Divine.

As I climb the third ladder, I say a prayer: "God willing, may this task I am about to do be a manifestation of 'Right Work.' May I be a servant to Your will."

The ultimate goal of *the work* is to find our true calling in the world, where our actions are infused with the peace and support of the Divine, whether we are "saving the world" or completing menial tasks. It's not *what* you do that matters, it's *how* you do it.

"*The work* is my path," I state as my mantra. "And right now, cleaning this chandelier is my greatest honor."

A glance at the hardwood floor thirty feet below suddenly makes my belly flip-flop. I feel a slight sway as I step onto the small platform on the highest scaffold, and tell myself, "I am not afraid of heights."

It's true. I'm not. Typically, I love heights. But, in a flash, I picture the scaffold folding beneath me, my head smashing on the floor, blood spreading in a pool around me. I whisper a prayer, "If I die doing this, at least I die serving *the work*. Please Animus: take me home." Fear floods through me and I can't shake the image. But I force myself into action.

Psychiatrist Robert Jay Lifton might surmise that this fear of annihilation arises from my totalistic dependence on the CTL creed: "I believe, therefore I am."

"I obey, therefore I am."

I take a deep breath. Below me is sacred space. Beneath this chandelier is where it all happens—where we gather for our most important work: the enactment of our dreams. This is where our truth, trapped in each dream, emerges from the dark unconscious into the light of day. This is where, with a subtle nod from Doug or an inner flash of inspiration, any one of us could be called to embody a dream role, to be a lioness, a brick wall, or a car careening out of control.

This is our chapel, our hearth. This is where the light settles when it streams in from the highest window, illuminating Doug as he speaks from a transparent podium, divine wisdom flowing through him. So many dreams of so many of my beloved CTL family members have been enacted here.

This is where Kim's pride of lions prowled, stalked, and circled her. On an invisible cue, they pounced in unison, devouring her and her silent screams, inviting each of us to experience dying to self.

This is where Jill and Paul stood, embodying Jill's dream of amputation. As husband and wife, they moved into each other in an armless embrace of exquisite tenderness. We all got to experience what it is to have no arms and to love. Intimacy does not require arms.

This is where Julie was held aloft and then crucified, as one of the three. Her courage and proximity to Christ incarnate brought some of us to tears.

This is where Kaylea and Sandy were strapped back-to-back, an "airplane" spinning wildly out of control, hit by enemy fire, then crashing in a powerful explosion. Gone. All gone. Until the first quivering sign of life appeared. A rebirth. An Easter blessing.

This is where Ashley was persecuted for her devotion to God. She was split in two when forced to sink onto a blade, slicing her from vagina to throat in one devastating thrust.

And this is where John J. stood for a suspended eternity, not knowing what to do with the cup offered him by an invisible hand. Finally, in a heart-rending gesture, he took a knee and drank. This moment of spontaneous devotion is emblazoned in my heart.

These images flash, galvanizing my focus on the task before me: polishing the chandelier that watches over *the work*. Tears slide down my cheek. I am filled with gratitude to Doug and Jenny for all they've done in creating this spiritual home on the mountain. The promise of inner growth through the transformational learning process, and through the holy theater of our dreams, is endless. Especially here.

I reach into my back pocket for the whiskbroom, then stretch on tiptoe to brush fuzzy dust from the chandelier's chain-link supports. I start at the top tier, moving systematically down to the smaller, lower links, letting the dust float like over-sized snowflakes to the floor below. I slide the whiskbroom back into my pocket with my left hand, while my right hand pulls a folded white cloth from the front pouch of my cleaning belt. My left hand, quick to the draw, has already pulled glass cleaner from its holster. I spritz the top tier of beveled glass, which cascades for over four feet, from top to tip.

I take a deep breath and settle in. This will take a while. As usual, I think it will take less time than it actually does. Two hours later, my altruism has faded.

Shit. I think. *I suck at glass. Always have. I wish Marie was here. We should be doing this together.*

"How's it going up there, G?!?" Gracie hollers from below.

I startle. I hadn't seen her enter. "Awesome!" The high pitch of my voice gives away my lie. "Hey, Grace," I shout. "Can you see streaks on the lower tier from down there?"

Pause. "Ahh . . . Yup!" she volleys back.

That was not the answer I wanted. I remind myself it is my privilege to clean this place. And that I am blessed to be trusted with this task. And I will stay at it until it is done right.

❧

Shortly after I got out of CTL, I was riveted by a news story about a small church in western New York, where two teenage brothers were beaten for twelve hours by fellow church members—including *both* boys' parents, their pastor, their sister, and a couple other members. One of the boys died, the other was profoundly injured. The congregants of that cultic church believed they needed to discipline the boys to induce them to repent their sins. Indoctrination was so complete that parental instincts were channeled to protect the church instead of the lives of their children.

Lifton says, "The dispensing of human existence is a flagrant expression of what the Greeks call *hubris*, of arrogant humans claiming to be God. Yet one underlying assumption makes this arrogance mandatory: the conviction that there is only one path to true existence, just one valid mode of being, and that all others are perforce invalid and false."[13]

Around the same time, an ex-devotee of Rajneesh told me over lunch, "If Rajneesh had asked me to kill someone, I would have done it."

Could I have gone that far if Doug had asked me? He didn't, so I will never know.

Death Valley

Late February, 2013

"IT'S JUST LIKE LIVING IN the cabin!" Sammy says, peeking from the camper's sleeping loft, watching Frank and me collapse our bed into side benches. I pause and smile at him.

"You're right. You get the high bed and we take the low one that folds!"

A few years earlier, we lived in the cabin in our backyard for a year and rented out our house to make money, hoping to avoid bankruptcy. Every morning, Frank and I would fold our bed into the living room couch before the kids and cats came tumbling down the steep stairs.

Lily, our hundred-pound dog, slept beside Frank and me. We loved living small. Four humans, two cats, and a dog lived in half the square footage we were used to. The smaller space brought us closer. Sammy was right. Camper life *is* a lot like living in the cabin. Except we have wheels.

Free from work stress on the road, our family's love starts flowing again as the miles roll away behind us. We play on beaches, climb mountains, and sing a hopeful blessing before meals at our tiny camper table. It's a far cry from the six-week road trip we'd dreamt about, but we accept and are grateful for our first-ever family vacation outside of weekend getaways in New England.

Looking out the windshield at the crashing waves and side-by-side campers, I smile. The trip came together like puzzle pieces falling into place: we leveraged thousands of dollars we'd accrued through cleaning services into the Hudson River Barter Network to book a camper for ten days; Frank found cheap tickets to LAX; and Frank and I were both awarded work scholarships for the CTL retreat at Eagle Spirit Institute—a prestigious retreat center on the California coast, where Doug and Jenny will be leading a retreat. The work scholarships cut retreat costs by a third.

The retreat is immediately after the kids' winter vacation from school, and a friend will pick them up from the airport and keep them until Frank and I return home four days later.

A whole week of just the four of us, followed by four days with Frank at Eagle Spirit! The stars are aligned, and I am feeling the power of God's love supporting our family and *the work*. I was surprised how quickly Frank agreed to go to Doug's retreat at Eagle Spirit, even though he'd stopped doing *the work* over a year ago. I love this about Frank. He doesn't hold grudges, and he's willing to do things for me when he knows how much it means. He stopped seeing Doug because he "wanted a break," but he still supports my ever-deepening commitment.

There is one disappointment, though: it's just too far out of the way for us to drive to the Grand Canyon, where my brother, Uncle Ray, hoped to meet us for a couple days. We settle for campgrounds along the California coast and a trip to Death Valley National Park.

On the fifth night of our vacation, after the kids are asleep, I show Frank my phone, which had been off all day while we played on the

Crystal Cove beach and hiked.

"I need you to read this. It's from Amy." I watch Frank's changing expression as he reads the text from my office manager.

"She left me a message, too—she's freaking out."

I start to cry. Frank puts down my phone and looks blankly at the blinking light from the camper's dashboard. "Did she say how much is needed?" he asks.

"No. Only that the bookkeeper was emphatic that we hold *all* paychecks until Monday, at least."

"Shit." Frank sighs. We lay side-by-side, minds and hearts whirling.

We are on vacation in California when I break the news to my staff over the phone the next morning that they won't be paid until Monday. I'm sick with shame and worry, and hope the stress is not too apparent to the kids.

With business pressures looming, camper life becomes claustrophobic. When we roll into Furnace Creek campground, I really need space—which is one thing Death Valley National Park delivers. The expanse is breathtaking, almost disconcerting.

I head off for a daylong Passage Quest and am relieved to be alone. I walk into the endless salt marsh, the sun bearing down, and set my sights on the dark, barren cliffs on the far side of the valley. The land that looked smooth and flat is cratered with dried-up streambeds. I scale up and down hundreds of rivulets, my feet crunching salt-crusted earth. After two hours of steady walking, I stop. The peaks I am walking toward appear farther away, not closer. I take in this metaphor.

The stable, profitable business I've put everything into for the past eight years looked enticing, but it's getting farther from my reach. Am I chasing an unattainable goal? Do I have what it takes to steer this business? Do I even want to?!? I scan the horizon and shift direction toward some creosote bushes, where I discover a meandering stream. I crawl into a thicket, seeking the only shelter from the sun for miles. I crouch beneath the bushes and write.

I reflect on all the changes I've enacted since buying Kim's cleaning business—adding auto detailing, carpet cleaning, and commercial cleaning. What started as a relatively straightforward residential cleaning business has become a complex monster. How did I get here? I begin to weep. I rage. I journal. I sing. I sigh. I journal some more. I sleep, and I listen.

It's time to get out of the cleaning business.

I try saying it out loud. It sounds real. I stand up and say it again.

"It's time to get out of the cleaning business."

Like a burden carried too long, its weight unnoticed, once laid down is a sweet, pleasant relief.

But not quite. I'm aware of the difficult road ahead of me, to close the business in a responsible way. I rise from my shelter, noting the lowering sun's rays, and return to my family to break the news. I'm not aware of the fact that this is a radical step for me—I am making a decision *without* Doug's help.

I knew Doug did not believe in the business any longer, and this has influenced me. At that time, however, all important decisions were made during my sessions with Doug. Was this a foreshadowing of the growing autonomy within me, incremental as it was?

"Oh, Mama. You have worked so hard and learned so much." Layla's eyes brim with tears after hearing my Passage Quest story. Frank shifts closer to me.

"I'm really proud of you," he says quietly, and looks deeply into my eyes as I allow his words to settle. I know he means it, both for what I have accomplished in these eight years, and for realizing it's time to let it go. Sammy is quiet, but I see the shine in his eyes. In many ways, he has taken the brunt of the burden, being forced to be alone far too often, far too young. Feeling their love and support for my decision quiets the shaming voices in my head.

"When will Uncle Ray get here?" Sammy's question helps us switch gears.

"Let's get the fire going," Layla chimes in and jumps into action.

"I can't believe he's really coming!" When I told Raymond we couldn't make it to the Grand Canyon, he was unphased and said, "Y'all are not gonna be that close without me setting eyes on those rascal kids of yours!"

"Jeez bro—I don't call a nine-hour drive 'close'!" But nothing would dissuade him. Besides, I was burning to see him.

He rolls into our campsite in a brand-spanking new, fully loaded, silver Titan pick-up truck.

"Did you finally bury that old brown Ford of yours?!?" I tease him, giving him a hug. He drove that Ford 150 for almost twenty years. This new rig seems to suit his new life as a mechanical engineer for the city of Chandler's waterworks. A high school dropout, Raymond was a laborer much of his life, and surprised us all by returning to school in his late thirties, eventually graduating and landing a job as a senior engineer.

Layla's fire is crackling, and within minutes, Ray's hilarious stories and the ensuing laughter start. His colorful life and big heart have turned him into a great storyteller. I hold my breath when he reaches into the cooler in the back of the truck, but relax when he offers everyone a Coke. He'd almost died during emergency back surgery when the doctors never thought to check his alcohol level; he went into withdrawal while under anesthesia. Ray was a heavy drinker at the time, but after surviving that, he swore off drinking.

Next morning, we all pile into his Titan and cruise Death Valley, awed by the vastness, the colors, the stark beauty. We hang out the windows, snapping photos, and the kids slide around in the truck bed. He intentionally speeds up at the corners, just enough to scare them—and me—but not enough to be dangerous.

We pull into the trailhead at Desolation Canyon, and the kids run ahead with Frank to check it out. Raymond and I walk together, savoring a brief bro-sis moment.

"How the hell are you doing? I mean, really?" This is his Big Brother, Tell-Me-the-Truth moment. "Is that business of yours still sucking you dry?"

I tell him of my decision to close the business. I tell him about Amy, at home with her little kids after working extra hard this week so I can be on vacation—and her paycheck still sitting in the lock box. I picture all my staff, freaked out about the sudden instability of their job.

We are quiet a moment, while my urge to cry again passes, taking in the rugged beauty of this canyon.

"Sounds like you're doing the right thing." He reaches out and squeezes my shoulder. "It ain't easy now, but life's gonna get easier for you."

I cry when we say goodbye, far too soon. We reiterate plans to not let so damn much time pass before our next visit. "I'll see y'all at Mole End this summer, and we'll catch some fish." A promise he'd been making for years.

"You stop growing, ya hear?" He jostles Sammy. "You better not be taller than me next time I see you!"

"And you, smarty pants, Miss Layla, are a damn good photographer. Don't you ever forget that," he says to Layla, who'd won his trust and respect using his Cannon.

Watching the taillights of his Titan fade into the vermillion cliffs, it does not occur to me that I might never see him again.

John

March 3, 2013

I PAUSE ON THE PATH, drinking in the expanse of the Pacific Ocean, and listen to the swish and crash of waves meeting the cliff below me. Eagle Spirit Institute is even *more* than its reputation foretold—more beauty, more peace, more dynamic. The ancient weaving of human and spiritual forces is palpable here, where people have retreated for decades to dive deep into spiritual realms while immersed in Nature's raw beauty.

Being here with my tribe *and* with Frank is an immeasurable gift. The crushing anxiety I'd felt days earlier around ending the cleaning business has lifted like a raven in flight. Nothing to worry about right now. I glance back along the empty path to see if Frank is approaching from the bathhouse. My stomach growls, so I continue to the dining hall, where he will find me.

I'm greeted by mouth-watering savory smells and scan the room to see a cluster of CTL friends standing, talking. My stomach tightens. Something is wrong. Sandy is crying. Others too. As I approach, Jenny steps toward me, reaching for my outstretched hand. She meets my questioning gaze and tells me, in a steady voice, "John J. committed suicide this morning. He jumped from the bridge at Milly's Falls."

I lurch backwards as a wail keens through me. My mind is on fire, picturing John's body falling, falling. *Why is he not here with us right now?!?*

Years ago, the town blocked off the bridge when they couldn't rally the funds to repair it properly and the lodge it was built to access went bankrupt. It spanned the Monarch River at a dizzying height—a cliff on one side, thickly wooded slope on the other. When I was in my early twenties, I worked at that lodge and walked across that bridge hundreds of times to access the little-known trail down to my favorite swimming hole. Every time, I'd stop at the midpoint and gaze into the swirling shallow waters, far below. Milly's Falls is more of a cascade than a waterfall, just downstream from the bridge. Over a hundred years ago, Milly, said to have been a promising local artist, took her life by leaping from this very spot. They say she can be seen on new-moon nights, rising from the black river, her gaze set on the stars above.

❧

Ai-Yi-Yi-Yai . . .
A woman's voice, keening. Visceral, embodied grief, rising from the core of the Earth, from the core of the woman.

I dreamt this, a week before our trip to California.

❧

I am sobbing. Jenny steadies me and I collapse into her arms. For the moment, I am not self-conscious, and am grateful for her strong embrace. Others arrive, and I gather myself to find Frank, who has just heard the news. We go outside to find quiet.

John and Kulomi, his lovely Albanian girlfriend, had lived in the cabin in our backyard as a partial barter exchange, just a few months earlier. There were projects begging for John's handyman skills, and we were delighted to be neighbors for their transition period; they needed privacy to figure out their trans-Atlantic relationship. We lived as good neighbors, passing each other in the driveway, sharing a few meals and friendly stories now and again.

"I didn't know. I didn't know." I keep repeating to Frank as we walk. He looks at me, eyes wide. "I didn't either," he says. He'd recently started a new position as a crisis clinician, learning the ropes, screening people for suicide ideation.

Stopping at an overlook, the tune *And When I Die* rises out of the wind. This song, made famous by Blood, Sweat & Tears, was penned by Laura Nyro, an impassioned songwriter whose too-short life was made rich by her lyrics.

I begin to sing into the ocean, salt spray mixing with my tears. Frank wraps his arms around me from behind, his emotion-filled voice joining mine, as John's had done at this past summer's retreat. John often leant his musical talent and generosity of spirit to CTL retreat participants who felt called to perform at an evening presentation. I had memorized every word of this song and belted them out with John beside me, but now, my voice caught on each line.

If it's peace you find in dying, well then, let the time be near . . .

John and I were two of the targeted ones. We stood together in our blindness. We sat at my kitchen table the week before he and Kulomi moved out of the cabin. We talked about practical matters, then I shared my homework and asked about his. John looked at me with surprise and asked, "Do you know what's going on with me?"

141

"No." I smiled, assuming he was referring to another screw-up. *I don't care about that shit, I love you for who you are. You are my brother. You don't say, and I don't ask.*

The vow of silence is an unspoken pact in controlling, hierarchical groups. If I'd broken it then, I would have learned that John was struggling with suicidal ideation. Instead, I behaved as one of Doug's good students, honoring not only the vow of silence, but also respecting the vow of distance. There were always at least a few degrees of separation between me and other CTL members. Doug controlled who was ready for what, when, and kept others one—or more—steps removed, but close by. Proximity soothes the worried mind. *Keep them close, but not—definitely not—in the know.* I didn't question. I had faith in a hierarchy I could not see. And cotton in my ears for everything but Doug's voice.

❧

Awake now, anguish ravages me, John, for not asking what you meant—what was going on with you. Had I been honest with myself and with you in that one moment, what might we have learned together?

Did you feel freedom during your free fall? Did your heart open, or were you simply terrified before hitting the cold, the stones that shattered every bone in your lower body? I imagine you pitching, face forward, into the water, peaceful now, letting the river's flow take you, washing you, accepting your blood, your broken body and whole heart. Water flows clear after it settles.

– Gerette's journal, March 3, 2013

❧

I cycle through disbelief, tears, and numbness before pulling myself together for the afternoon retreat session. Frank and I decide it would be best to not be in the same small group, giving us space to do our own inner work. We hug outside the large white building where my group is meeting. I step into the space to join my CTL family, most of whom traveled from New England for this special retreat. I believe I am exactly where I need to be, and trust that together we will find peace.

❧

Five years into my post-cult healing, I'm sitting across from John's longtime partner, who he'd spent a decade with prior to Kulomi, untangling strands of memories that still sting like salt on open wounds. We open doors others prefer to keep closed and ask each other: Was Doug responsible for John's death? Either way, we acknowledge the complexity. I learn that John's family of origin has faced suicide before. And we don't forget the good stuff: the insight, the love, the camaraderie. We talk about blind faith in the CTL doctrine, the belief that it would save our souls, while it emptied our pockets both literal and proverbial, bankrupting our reality.

We come to no conclusions. It is a messy pile unraveled between us, our tea cups nearly empty. I pause, taking a last sip, and notice that I feel calm. In anticipation of the conversation, I'd been anxious. But once the words were spoken, there was room for nuance, complexity, and the unknown. This settled my nervous system and allowed me to breathe. Truth lives beyond the blinders of yes and no, right and wrong, out in the open where it can be seen, listened to, and felt.

Raymond

January 8-9, 2014

IT'S 7 A.M., THE PHONE rings and my mind lurches to Columbia Memorial Hospital, where Mom had double knee replacement surgery the day before.

"It's for you," Frank says, handing me the phone with one eyebrow raised.

The night before, we were assured that the surgery had been successful, and that Mom would take her first steps within twenty-four hours. But we did anticipate that she'd be vulnerable for quite a while. Her only brother, my beloved uncle, had died two days before Christmas, sitting in his favorite chair with a wrapped Christmas present for his unborn granddaughter at his feet.

Kin quietly passes life's torch. Shock, grief, and Christmas cheer mingled and confounded us through the Holy Nights. Pre-op procedures prevented Mom from attending the celebration of his life: a feast and heart-felt sharing at an Irish pub in downtown Ithaca. My bag from that trip still sits on the floor of my bedroom.

I've worried that Mom will soon fall apart from grief and stress, and as I take the phone from Frank, I assume this is the moment. But I couldn't be more wrong.

"Hello." At first, I only hear a choking sound, and then an explosion of words that made no sense.

"It's . . . It's about Ray . . ." I sit down, feeling sudden gravity. Suze, my brother's new girlfriend, is incoherent, but certain words stand out.

"Hit head . . . Fell."

In my pajamas, I hover next to the woodstove, leaning my bottom on its radiant soapstone top. I shiver, my gaze fixed on the scene outside our bay window, trying to understand what Suze is saying.

"They said he might not make it."

Outside, dazzling white stretches past the frame of pine branches, a crystalline early-January landscape. How many times have I gazed at this familiar view out my living room window? Not enough. I've denied myself that opportunity by keeping my nose to the grindstone, year after weary year, hardly entering this room that is supposed to be for living. I rediscovered this room after getting out of the cleaning business, when I was finally able to recognize my home as refuge, the view from my un-lived-in living room window quickly morphs into my favorite meditation, with hands wrapped around a steaming cup of tea. This frame captures our property's humble complexity. Robust, with the promise of Earth's bounty now stilled by deep winter's steady hand, it holds our large, rambling vegetable garden, bee hives, chicken yard, and small swamp. Beyond that, hardwood forest rises up the east-facing slope.

My vision is drawn to the center point, the field beyond the garden where the wind runs free and birds fly, dipping wingtips to catch light from the rising sun. Inside and outside this bay window lives a balance of the wild and cultivated, an expression of our family's striving within the greater context of Nature.

Viewing all of this is not luxury, but sustenance, at times more necessary than food.

Suze's sobs begin to settle as I cling to the Hearthstone's steady warmth, but the stone does not warm me. Nothing can warm me as I comprehend that Raymond, my one and only brother, my Big Bro Ray, fell when he was drunk last night, hit his head, and may not make it.

Alcoholism. I rarely thought about it. While doing *the work*, addiction was viewed as separation from God. Depending on your view, alcoholism can either be a tragic disease or a personal disorder. In one modal you get to be a victim, and in the other, the cause. How does this framework change if we think of addiction in relation to the "inner authoritarian," as Alstad and Kramer write about in *The Guru Papers*?

Once trapped in a good-or-bad mindset, we lose the vast majority of choices that lay in life's nuance, in the hundreds of words for love, in the unending and ever-changing pulse of life. For eighteen years, I strove to squelch my "bad" self and boost my "good." Outside that cocoon, I became more human again. Did my brother drink for the sweet release of getting away from the clamoring voice of his good or bad self? "Enough already! Let me drown you, bitch!"

Ray chose the bottle, and I my guru. But why should he die and I live?

Walking into Mercy Hospital the next morning, I get a text from Kat: He is dead. Just twenty-four hours after the hysterical phone call from Suze. I stop in the glassed-in walkway between the parking garage and the hospital, catching my breath, silently watching the slow rise of the January sun into a still, cloudless sky. My brother is dead.

My mother is inside this building, recovering from surgery. Two weeks ago, she suddenly lost her only brother. Today, I have lost mine. I search my mind for my current homework and can't find it. I'm on my own. *The work* can't help me. I take another breath, exhale slowly, and walk into the hospital to tell Mom that her son is dead.

❧

My sister Katherine's capacious home becomes the gathering place, as family members heed the call to be together. Jules is resting in the easy chair in front of the fireplace, her feet up, eyes puffy. She startles, looks up at us, and wails.

"I want my brother back! I want him back *right now*." She begins to rock, and her fervor grows. "It's not *fair*! He should be here with us, with all of us *right* now!"

Her sobs choke her, pierce our hearts. We sisters move in to comfort her. We reach out, touch her shoulder, caress her hand, stroke her baby-fine silver hair. Jules, third oldest, is special in a way that defies the hierarchy of age, making all of us her big sisters. Clara grabs tissues and passes them around. But it's Kat who finds her voice.

"Ya know, Jules, we all want him back. But now we have to find him in different ways." We nod and murmur, and blow our noses.

"Besides," Kat continues, "look outside—it's January in New York state. This is the *last* place he'd want to be anyway, right?" We chuckle, grateful for a smile. "I heard there is a record high in Arizona today. It's perfect he leaves in such heat."

When Dad walks in that evening, he is a broken man. He can barely walk, his sobs taking over his fragile frame. When I was a kid, he felt like a big man, but now, I have to suppress the impulse to pick him up and cradle him.

Sonny and Rosie, cousins from Long Island, show up with lobster-and-five-cheese ravioli, handmade at the Italian deli near their home. They are the salve we need, the Italian blood that flows through all of us, linking our sorrow and freeing our heavy hearts. The aroma of sauce and steam rises from big pots, softening the stuck places inside as we huddle around the island in Kat's kitchen.

There are plenty of tears, but also laughter and a feeling of something that I cannot name. Have I ever experienced this? It is a feeling of unity, despite despair. It is the feeling of shared loss, of deepest vulnerability that, in the act of moving toward each other, frees us from old, well-worn patterns and invites new synapses to form, new light to fill the ragged cracks. At the time, my mind is still tightly wrapped in CTL doctrine, and I have no words for this feeling. Six years later, as I write these words, I realize this feeling was Love.

Love rises from those ravioli pots and urges us awake. Love swoops in to fill the empty holes of our grief. The love that was sparked between our parents, sprinkled into our DNA, and linked us as a family—this love, this dynamic-but-ephemeral love flows through me and, I daresay, each one of us that evening. An invisible hand stitches a new tapestry from the old frayed one as ragged folds of time collapse and disappear. A synergy swirls around those steaming pots, while friendly familial spirits visit from their graves, blessing our clan who, for once, can be at peace together. Hope kindles out of our collective loss, and our fragmented family comes together in a new way, perhaps preparing us for the storm that is yet brewing.

Suze sets the date for Raymond's funeral in Arizona at the same time as the first-ever CTL Arts Retreat, which flows into the annual Winter Retreat—if you attend both, a full week of being immersed in *the work.*

I panic. Torn loyalty has teeth, snapping at erroneous threads, desperate for something to sink into. I begin talking with my sisters, father, and mother, and hatch a plan to relieve me of having to choose between my birth family and my CTL family.

I latch onto my father's frailty; he can't possibly fly alone. Kat will accompany him to Phoenix, and since he wants to stay for a week or two, I will fly out *after* the funeral to accompany him on the return flight. Besides, we want to have a service in New York state once Mom is mobile again, so it doesn't seem to matter if I miss the official funeral.

I tell my family I've already paid for the retreat; no need to mention the payment plan. Doug taught me that white lies are acceptable, and in fact sometimes create harmony when talking with people who are not likely to understand the mysterious ways of the divine. Doug supports the plan for me and I am elated, as it allows me to attend both retreats *and* be a helpful, conscientious daughter. But the fact remains: I will miss my brother's funeral.

I dive into the Arts Retreat, painting, singing, and dancing my way through my grief, and then transition to the big Winter Retreat, creating a weeklong cocoon to dwell in *the work* as I grieve. Through a flurry of emails and a couple phone conversations, I become aware of a rift forming between my father and my sisters. Being in an altered state, complicit with my chosen family, I am unable to reckon with this reality. What really took place for me up at The Farm that week, I can only piece together from my limited journal entries. My actual memories are notably dim. For instance, I wrote:

I get lost, buffeted by the gusty winds of my sisters as they expose their wounds that get projected onto Dad.

My blind loyalty to Doug originated with my staunch defense of my father, who I believed could do no wrong. I was brought up with the old-school belief of revering the father, even when he defiled what is true. I carry this torch forward through Doug's teaching.

Oh, how these birth family voices shut me down, take me out and away from my own family here in the mountains, here in God's love.

Pitting birth family against "pure" family is as old as the first cult. It is a cruel hand of humanity that forces, or subtly encourages, choosing one over the other.

My homework, coming out of this transformational retreat, is to be living with my archetypal family. When I notice the dirt outside the door and feel my compulsion to sweep, I need to turn to the Doctor, to receive His injection of archetypal poison that will flow into my entire body, returning me home to the Trinity. Feel the delight as He gives me the injection.

If this is not a recipe for dissociation, what is?

～

My plan fails. My father flies home unaided, and we never have a memorial service in New York state. Our family, as we knew it, unravels beyond recognition, and what little grasp I have on it crumbles in confusion. Dad spouts bitterness, so similar to his rants about Mom years ago, now replacing her with my sisters as the object of his spite. I seek refuge in the only thing I trust, making plans for two CTL retreats, one in Connecticut, the other in Canada.

It is never possible to know how one twist in a sequence of events might change a course completely. Had I attended Raymond's funeral, could I have prevented some of what unfolded? Or would my fragile psyche have made things even worse? Who or what caused this family volcano to erupt? Was it simply its time, the dysfunction of our family having grown to a crisis point? How much was the eruption nursed by an outside force, a snake who lay quietly in the grass? Through Raymond's final days and the stormy months that followed, she was coiled, ready to strike and to retreat without a trace. Her poison worked quickly, while she lay in the sun, flicking her forked tongue.

PART FOUR

SNAPPING

"snap/'snap/ vb snapped; snapping:
to break suddenly; to grasp at something eagerly;
to give way suddenly under strain; to emit sparks and
flashes, i.e. 'eyes snapping with fury';
to capture or take possession of suddenly; to break suddenly:
to break short or in two;
to make or do without preparation or delay.
snap adj.: unusually easy or simple"

– Merriam-Webster[14]

Shock

May 27, 2014

IN MY NEW ROUTINE, I only check email in the morning and again after lunch. Time management has never been my forte, but I've decided it's never too late to try. No longer tethered to the cleaning company, I am pecking away at improving our guest cabin, long-neglected projects in our home, and odd jobs in bookkeeping and occasional house cleaning.

My morning teacup in hand, I read dozens of CTL emails before getting to Michael's resignation. I am stunned and sad. It seems so out of the blue that he would decide to leave right now, when momentum for *the work* is growing. But I've read so many "Leaving CTL" letters over the years, I've grown to trust the tides of change. I remind myself that I left CTL, too—for a couple months, when demands with the cleaning company were just too much—and it was helpful for my inner process.

Many who've left return in six months or a year, even just six weeks, newly invigorated and ready to renew commitment to furthering *the work* in the world. I think of Doug's "revolving door"—his declaration that people can join and leave CTL as they desire—as an example of the generosity of spirit that is a hallmark of our organization. I send Michael a personal message, wishing him well in the next chapter of his inner work, close my computer, and turn to the mound of linens that need mending and stain removal.

A couple hours later, the phone rings. It's Gracie—I've got a list of things to talk with her about. I pin the phone between my right shoulder and chin, clothespin in hand and an empty laundry basket at my feet.

"Hey, Grace! Just give me a sec—I just have to get this last pillowcase on the line. You can't believe how sweet it is for me to be home, doing these simple—" But Gracie cuts me off.

"Hey, G. Did you hear?"

Her tendency to cut me off doesn't bother me today. I'm doing exactly what I need to be doing, feeling the Animus with me as I stitch and scrub.

"Yeah. I read Michael's email. I'm bummed to see him go." I glance at my white sheets, fluttering in the breeze. Gracie and I have worked closely with Michael for years on numerous building-related projects. "It's going to be tough finding someone to fill his shoes up at The Farm, but I'm sure someone will step up to the plate. I bet he'll be back before too long."

I walk back into the house and my stomach growls. I scan the kitchen, wondering if I can make some lunch while chatting with Gracie.

"Uhh . . . sounds like you *didn't* hear." Gracie pauses, her voice quiet on the other end of the line. "You need to go back to your email. They all left."

"What? What are you talking about?!? *Who* left?!?" I run up the stairs, turn on my computer, and begin to see. Scanning the list of new CTL emails, I feel the Earth beneath me tilting in slow motion. I read Kaylea's resignation email. Then Willy's. Oh, my God, Agatha is leaving too?!? And Sandy?!? *What the fuck?*

My world slants sideways, and I am falling, falling, falling. Even Ann, oh my God. *Ann* is leaving CTL! All six of the head teachers for the Center for Transformational Learning are leaving the organization. Each is resigning for reasons they carefully explain in their individual emails. Each naming all the normal reasons for leaving:

"My inner work, blah, blah, blah."

"My homework is to blah, blah, blah."

"My dreams are telling me blah, blah, blah."

But not one of them says anything about why they are leaving together. I'm unaware of hanging up the phone. I read and reread the emails, searching for some hidden key. I pace from my computer to my window, back and forth. I pound my fists on my computer desk, and the monitor shakes. I burst into tears when Frank gets home.

"I'm in shock," I tell him. He encourages me to go for a walk. I walk. I cry. I take deep breaths that explode on the exhale. And I keep repeating to myself, "I'm in shock."

> *shock*: N: 1) disturbance in the equilibrium or permanence of something. 2) a sudden or violent disturbance of the mind, emotions, or sensibilities.
>
> – Merriam-Webster[15]

I'm feeling it's *and*, not *or*: A violent disturbance of the mind, emotions, *and* sensibilities.

Doug and Jenny each send emails with calm reassurances and words about the future, but even this does not address the rupture of today.

As evening falls, a storm moves in from the north. Skies darken, lights flicker, and heavy raindrops plunk one by one on my window pane as I write and send this short email to all CTL members. I hit send just before the power goes out.

Dear Michael, Sandy, Kaylea, Willy, Ann, and Agatha,

It has been a huge day, reading Michael's email first . . . then all of your emails. My world stopped turning as I read them, each with your specific, individual words about why you need to leave CTL right now. WTF? Is there CTL without you? I don't know. I'm in shock. But not one of you said why you are leaving all at the same time. I thought we were an organization based on autonomy. Why then this group exodus? What is going on here?!? Tomorrow evening, we will come together for one last time, as the Executive Committee that is no more. The rest of us will carry on, as best as we can. But I sincerely hope, in our circle tomorrow evening, that you can help me to understand why you are all leaving as a group.

I need you. And I love you. You are my family of families. I understand you are leaving CTL, but trust this core of togetherness will never die. My heart is breaking. And I know Doug would say this kind of breaking is good. And I feel the Animus is right here with me, doing my dishes as I write, stroking my hair as I cry, staying with me as I gaze off dissociated as this storm rolls in. He is right here with me.

I feel you, my brothers and sisters, on this stormy night, shining like stars above the clouds.

Love,
Gerette

Years later, preparing this manuscript, I realize that I broke all the CTL email-writing rules when I sent that email. I addressed specific people (only leaders were allowed to do this), confronted them (Doug alone can do this), did not even mention my homework (Rule #1), much less include my carefully written dreams (Rule #2). Sacrilege.

The autonomy I felt lacking in their collective act of severance awakened my own. Their ambivalence forced me into alertness. Once my mind latched onto this question—why the group exodus?—there was no rest for me. Nothing short of comprehending why they left together would satisfy me. I was a tomcat on the prowl, both predator and preyed upon, circling and circling but never finding a mouse to pounce on. It was inconceivable to me that the organization itself was flawed, even less so that the leadership was unscrupulous. That awareness, however, would come soon enough.

Last Exec

May 28, 2014

WORDS, WORDS, WORDS. BUT NOTHING is making sense. For an hour and a half, twenty of us sit in the classroom where we've sat together every Wednesday evening for years now, for Executive Committee. People are talking and talking, but I still do not hear the answer to my question. Why the hell did six leaders of CTL—esteemed leaders, the core of the organization; who were closest to Doug; who'd been trained by, loved by, and lived by Doug's inspiration, year after year—why, *oh why*, did they decide to leave in one fell swoop?

One foul swoop.

I listen, but there is something they are not saying. Or I am not hearing.

Five minutes before the end of the meeting (we always end on time), Kaylea speaks, in her quiet, naked voice, the truth I need to hear. When I first met her years ago at a brunch for women in *the work*, she reminded me of a deer—timid and fragile, fear stitched into the sage-and-beige skirt she wore, hoping to blend into the woodwork.

She barely spoke until she read a poem about irises, her voice shaking: ". . . in my hand, wild blue iris, earth-bound sky, a blaze of yellow. Joy lives on the tongue of grief, grace in a heedless world."

Newly freed from a traumatic marriage, *the work* had become her lifeline. Over the years, her trembling calmed and her passion allowed her to rise through the ranks of CTL leadership, landing as one of its top teachers. Kaylea's innate wisdom, artistry, and poetry was woven into the public face of CTL, her generosity of spirit so great it was difficult to see.

Now, she speaks. "Doug called me sometimes and berated me for an hour, sometimes two hours at a time. He would yell and yell. I could hardly speak. One hour. Two hours. Sometimes more. This happened not once, not twice, but several, no—many times."

Her words, precise and bearing no hidden meaning, are the truth that jolts my sleeping conscience awake. An irreparable crack in the veneer of my mind forms from her words, allowing my own sense of justice to rise. In the minute it takes her to say her piece, my psyche begins to reorganize around one undeniable fact in direct conflict with what I had *believed* to be true: that Doug was spiritually perfect.

In the hushed silence that follows the moment Kaylea's words leave her mouth, my world reorders. For Doug to yell at Kaylea for hours at a time, even minutes at a time, pierces my heart and dethrones Doug from the untouchable pedestal my psyche placed him on so many years ago. No one—not even Doug—should be allowed to hurt Kaylea. A fierce mama-bear awakens in me, swinging.

But the meeting is not over. Two minutes left. Michael says, "Don't worry"—he is trying to reassure us of something, but his words do the opposite—"Sandy and I have decided to host a summer retreat at our place."

An alarm with loud buzzing noises and flashing lights sets off in my head. I start to sweat, heart pounding, hands shaking. I blurt, "How

can you do this?!? You are making us choose between *you* and Doug?!?"
My voice verges on hysteria. The summer retreat plans for The Farm
are well underway, set to be our best one yet.

From the other side of the room, Willy speaks quietly, gently.
"Maybe, Gerette, you don't have to choose."

This is the point in my story where listeners divide into two camps:
those who have experienced and become free from cultic abuse, and
those who haven't. Those who haven't look at me blankly and ask,
"What's the big deal about hearing 'maybe you don't have to choose'?"

❧

At sixteen, I don't have a choice, even though they ask me "Who do
you want to live with?" I am furious with Mom, who set these wheels
in motion. I lean my head against the angled wooden slats of the
headboard of my bed and look out the window. Across from me, a row
of blue and red ribbons are taped to the wall—relics of my younger self
in the sheep barn at Duke County Fair. The compartment behind my
back holds my diaries, pens, pencils, a dried daisy, and a wishing stone
I found beside the duck-weed pond. Its white ring was green until I
scrubbed it clean.

I don't take out my diary or my stone. My arms are crossed, but I
refuse to cry. *How can she do this to us?*

I don't remember choosing what to take with me into my new life
with my father and sister, Clara, six-hours away, to New York's Finger
Lakes region. But once the plan is in place, a flame stirs within me. I
cut my hair short and get a perm. Dismayed by tight afro curls instead
of gentle waves, I get a black derby and wear it every day.

Frye boots and cufflinks come next. Thus, I walk into my new life
having shed the old one. The freedom to choose to be whoever I want

delights me. No one knows I don't dance, so I dance. No one knows I don't do theatre, so I become a thespian. No one knows my mother initiated the divorce, so I begin to love her again, slowly.

Why was the divorce such a shock to me? They'd been fighting for months. Ruthlessly. The cows were gone. Dad took a job out of state and commuted home when he could. Our Walton-style family existed only in my mind, which refused to acknowledge the decay visible both on our front porch and between our parents.

∝

There must have been indications of CTL's erosion, too, but in my conscious mind at least, I trusted Doug and the CTL organization completely.

Until I didn't.

Part Five

WAKING UP AGAIN AND AGAIN

"The breezes at dawn have secrets to tell you
Don't go back to sleep!
You must ask for what you really want.
Don't go back to sleep!
People are going back and forth
Across the doorsill where the two worlds touch,
The door is round and open
Don't go back to sleep!"

– Rumi, translated by Coleman Barks, *Essential Rumi* [16]

Gerette Buglion

"If grief can be a doorway to love, then let us all weep for the world we are breaking apart,
so we can love it back to wholeness again."
–Robin Wall Kimmerer, *Braiding Sweetgrass*[17]

It Is Over

GRACIE, SITTING DIRECTLY ACROSS FROM me, sees it happen. She watches me snap out of CTL. "It was like a light turned on," she later said.

Maybe you don't have to choose echoes in my ear as I quietly leave the meeting to drive home. *Maybe you don't have to choose* beats in my heart as I turn north on Route 122, driving through the Wisner Woods. *Maybe you don't have to choose* seeps into every cell as I stretch my night vision, attentive to the wandering moose. *Maybe you don't have to choose* fills my breath, steady and surprisingly calm.

Arriving home, I stand, as I often do, at the edge of my driveway facing due east. I feel into the expanse of woods and water between me and The Farm. The stars are brilliant overhead, and I feel my feet on the Earth. Her springtime pulse is as quiet and steady as my own heart, beating into the night.

Then, I hear the words "It is over" spoken aloud by a source I cannot name. Again, "It is over." I'm not startled. What is over for

167

me? *Let me count the ways*:

> 1) Believing I have to choose, and that in choosing, I am betraying one side or the other—It is over.
> 2) The CTL rules that I have needed, that I have clung to—It is over.
> 3) Protecting and insulating myself from Doug, each one of the teachers, and my fellow members—It is over.
> 4) Putting the leadership team on a pedestal and keeping myself less-than. It is over.

It is not *the end*, though. In fact, I hear a quiet, murmuring song of beginning. I don't know the lyrics yet, or the tune. But I am listening. Before turning toward the porch light of home, I stand and listen some more.

A flood of grief and a visceral sensation of *Frank* washes over me. How much have I projected my own darkness onto him; how much he has taken the brunt of my protecting, and insulating, and rule clinging, and believing that I must choose?

A dam breaks. The dam that has been holding my Self from myself, from my home and my marriage. I weep with the gushing waters and see the truth: I have treated CTL as more important than my home, my children, and my husband! There is a fundamental way that I have not cared for them, and this *not caring* is over. Because I do care. I care, and I want to show up—especially where I am needed the most—in my own home and family. I go inside and shake Frank awake.

Oftentimes, when my emotions are high, my words tumble out in a messy pile. Not tonight. Sitting in our tiny guest room and whispering so as not to wake the kids, I articulate my awakening.

Frank's eyes fill, and tears catch the lamplight. "I've been waiting for this."

We collapse into each other's arms as silent heaves wash through us.

❧

In 1990, when Frank and I bought the house that is still our home today, a large patch of forget-me-nots bloomed in scattered patches all over the wide lawn, tucked in amongst the ferns along the garage, and in other random places.

At that time, I was deep in my career as a Waldorf teacher. I co-created and taught a weekly class for three-year-olds and their moms and/or dads. The simplicity of this once-a-week activity was its brilliance, and it was fertile ground for the most fun I'd had in my nineteen years of teaching. At the end of one school year, I was inspired by the prolific forget-me-nots blooming in early June, and dug up clumps, put them in small pots, and gave them to each parent-child pair as a goodbye present.

A few years later, I ran into one of these parent/child teams at the grocery store. The three-year-old towhead had grown into a lanky youth. They told me, with a twinkle in their eyes, that they'd planted the forget-me-nots beside their house, and every spring when they bloom, they greet them—calling them "Gerette-me-nots." It breaks me still to recall such sweetness.

"Deep in their roots, all flowers keep the light."
– Theodore Roethke, "Unfold! Unfold!"[18]

I had a tidiness habit that encompassed the outdoors. I used to mow compulsively, trying to create tidy places for flowers. You can't call it gardening—it was more like managing. The thing about forget-me-nots is, they're not tidy—they bloom wherever the heck they want, and they don't stay put. In my ignorant quest for order, I wiped out the forget-me-nots with the mower. I'd look for them in the spring, and nada. Nowhere to be seen. For years. Until the morning after my night with the stars, after the last executive meeting.

There, beside the rotting corner boards of my house, was a large and hardy patch of forget-me-nots. The memory of Gerette-me-nots flowed with my grateful tears. On the first day of my renewed life, I write a long letter to CTL leadership, what is left of it, and to the membership at large, letting them know that I am done with:

> Protecting Doug and CTL leaders.
> Believing that I have to choose between CTL and anything else.
> Following rules just because they are there.
> Putting anyone on a pedestal and keeping me lower than, less-than.
> It is over.

On the second day of my new life, I decide to leave CTL completely, and in my resignation letter, I tell the recipients it is time for me to tend my home and my family, and to enjoy the Gerette-me-nots that grow wherever the heck they want to. This time, I do not say anything about returning. Instead, I walk over to Elizabeth's home to clean.

After closing the cleaning company, I made a pact with myself to only take on cleaning clients that I could walk to. The walk helps calm me, but I'm relieved when no one is home. I start dusting; the pale-purple microfiber swallows a fine layer of dust from the broad coffee table. I glance up to check for cobwebs, and as I reach into my back pocket for my feather duster, a buzz in my apron pocket startles me. Digging my phone out from the folded cleaning cloths, I see that it's

Val, Pearl's friend who I first met at her Mother's Blessing years ago, who recently joined Executive Committee. I answer immediately. I put her on speakerphone while I whisk dog hairs off the sofa.

Val has become one of my favorite people in CTL—her creativity, intensity, and levity is a joy to be around. She owned a small gym, and I was thrilled when she asked if, freed from managing my unwieldy business, I'd be interested in a part-time job managing hers. I readily agreed to one day a week, and enjoyed the challenge of applying my hard-earned business skills.

I'm grateful to hear her voice.

"Holy shit, Gerette," Val's voice is filled with agitation and concern. "Last night I was thinking about, well—do you remember that retreat when Doug had Brad strangle you?"

"Yeah, Val. I know. I can't get it out of my mind," I said. "Not only that, he made me repeat that story every single retreat after that. Do you think . . . ?" I am shaking as I speak, but I can't finish my sentence. I move into the kitchen to start on the counters.

Val whistles slowly. "Jeez, Gerette. This is so fucking intense!"

This exchange is the first time someone from within CTL acknowledges there was anything wrong with how I was treated.

"Let's talk more later, Val. I've got to focus here." I was shaking again, and wasn't sure when Elizabeth would return home. "Thanks for reaching out, sis . . . Hey, I love you." Dropping to my knees, I wipe cooking grease from the smooth, slate-gray cupboard, and begin heaving silently.

On the third day of my new life, I wake up knowing I am done with Doug as my analyst. Telling him this is actually easy. In a one-minute phone call, I say, "Hey, Doug, I just want you to know I've decided to take a break from sessions with you."

"No problem," he says with breezy confidence. "I'm here for you

171

whenever you want." I am relieved by the ease of such a monumental change, but also unsettled by the lack of fanfare. I wonder if he will miss me.

Later that day, I talk with Doug about the paid bookkeeping work I am doing for him, and we decide I'll continue doing it, at least for now. We discuss the terms and parameters of my working for him, and I am amazed: for the first time, I am speaking to him without the haze of trauma-projection and power-over authority.

"Do you still want to leave your checking account deposits on the dining room table?" I did not need to complete the question with "since I'm no longer your client." We both knew where the question was coming from.

"Sure," he said. "No need to change a system that is working." His voice was subdued. After hanging up the phone, I realize that, at least for the moment, he needs me. Taxes are due.

On the fourth day of my new life, I begin to write and organize my experiences. I explore the nature of my relationship to Doug and start to recognize disturbing inequities. Through my journaling and talking with Frank, I say the word *cult* for the first time, in first person.

I was in a cult.

In writing this phrase, "Today I am released from a cult," I feel enormous relief. I don't really know what it means; I feel the truth of it.

On the fifth day of my new life, I go for a ride.

Riding Home

June 1, 2014

OUR RIDE, PLANNED A WEEK ago, was based on a stellar weather forecast. Sue has been building me up to it. A biking neophyte, I am grateful for Sue's coaching. I'm determined to join my daughter Layla for the final four days of her cross-country bike trip, just two weeks away. Sue has been breaking me in with six-to-ten-mile rides that gradually increase in both difficulty and length. She says I am now ready for the thirty-six-mile Sagamore Lake ride. The day dawns as bright as the forecast said it would.

I am terrified. Not about the ride. I am scared about being with people who are not part of the CTL bubble. I have not yet spoken to a single outside person since my resignation. I force myself to go on the ride, despite my impulse to cancel.

Sue and Sylvie arrive early to pick me up. My hands visibly shake as I load my bike onto their rack. I fumble with my gear, spilling it and myself into the back seat of their car, not knowing how I'll make it through this day. Can I be honest with them? Can I actually do this ride without being transparent about the fact that I am a changed person?

Sylvie and I have been in a women's group together for more than twenty years. Inspired by the film *Dead Poets Society*, our ragtag group started meeting once a month to read poetry and tell stories. A core group of us have remained after others drifted away, and we've shifted into a support group: The Seven Sisters.

For years, each of us took turns facilitating activities ranging from making plaster masks, reading books together, and hosting Mother's Blessing ceremonies. The monthly meetings faded after two of our seven moved out of state, but we've maintained twice-annual, three-day gatherings.

I wonder if I can tell Sue and Sylvie about my major change at the same time, since I don't know Sue as well, but as we turn west onto Route 101, I lean forward from the back seat, still shaking, and rest my elbows on their bucket seats. I open my mouth and words spill out, sometimes accompanied by tears. I tell them about Kaylea speaking at the meeting, and how the dam broke within me. I describe what happened when I arrived home and stood in my driveway that night, and how I went inside to wake Frank. I describe the leak of recognition that sprouted into a cleansing river, washing me away from Doug and the Center for Transformational Learning.

"That powerful grip on my mind, on my psyche, is broken. And I have my life back," I conclude, and sit back in my seat to take a deep breath.

Sue, a woman of few words, utters a resounding, "Holy Shit! Gerette!"

Sylvie is quiet. When I see that she is wiping tears, mine start up again. I notice I am not shaking any more. Telling them what happened, letting my body shake but talking anyway, was a tonic for my nervous system.

The best part, and perhaps most therapeutic of all, is getting on my bike to ride. My legs moving, deep breaths, and the sensation of air, sun, and wind all combine into a wondrous, integrative, magical pill. I enter a stretch of road where I am on my own, Sue way ahead of me and Sylvie trailing. I need solitude.

I labor through a long, slow uphill, then meet the wide wooded curve that opens to the stunning expanse of a long view of Sagamore Lake. I fly downhill toward its pristine shore while my heart bursts with the release. I am alive, and in my body, and in the center of my life again—for the first time in too many years to count.

At the far end of the lake we take a break, and my phone picks up enough signal for a text from Doug to come through. When I see the text, I feel compelled to respond. I go off to find a bathroom—a place of safety I often seek when I need privacy. I fuss over how to respond to his message. I type and delete and type some more, and the shaking starts again.

Sylvie checks in with me, because they are ready to head out. I reluctantly tell her I'm trying to respond to a text from Doug. She gently suggests that perhaps it could wait, that I don't need to respond right now.

This is a radical concept for me.

※

It is time to rediscover myself, and I need my friends in a whole new way. Marina welcomes me back, judgment free, after my snapping out. She offers her wisdom and resources. She hands me a multi-volume CD set called *The Neurobiology of We*, by Daniel Seigel, MD. Listening to these CDs helps me understand some of the neurological processing occurring within me as I heal, whether I am conscious of it or not.

In his book, *Mindsight*, Siegel writes "[. . . W]e can change our lives by developing a 'coherent narrative,' even if we did not start out with one."[19] He describes how the *process* of creating a lucid description of one's traumatic experience helps to "rewire" the brain's anatomy as it was before the trauma was experienced. My post-cult mind finds this concept revelatory, and very hopeful. Just talking about, or writing, or engaging in some creative expression about the difficult experiences will—in and of itself—open new information pathways in the brain!

I did not know it at the time, but my bike ride around Lake Sagamore, sharing my story with friends, was rewiring neural pathways in my brain, promoting physical healing from my traumatic experiences. Movement, talking, trembling, even my backward slip with that text to Doug, were affirmative steps forward on my days-old journey of healing from mind control.

Waking Up
Again and Again

WHEN I ANSWER THE PHONE, a man with a heavy accent asks for me. "Is dis, mize Ger . . . Garret B . . . ooglon?"

"Who is this?" I am curt, ready to hang up.

"I vas medi-tating und dis name und number show me. No vorry. I have nozing to sell. Only blessing."

"Who are you? How did you get my number?" Alarm and curiosity in equal parts awaken.

"I vas medi-tating und ze spirit diret me. Dis number. I have nozing to sell. Would you like to veceive a blessing? No vorry. Only blessing." A dozen more rounds of questioning circles back to the same assurance: Only blessing.

His exotic accent. How much harm can there be in a blessing?

You have to get them to follow your instructions—this creates investment, enhances belief. I open my cupboard and take out a candle, as he asks me to. The smooth coolness of the candle meets my skin and I wake up.

"What else do you offer?" I ask. He talks about his book, his retreats. I hang up the phone, palms and pits wet with sweat. I'm pissed.

~

I dream of a deer running straight toward me. I stretch out my hands. As the deer passes by, my hands touch its head, then neck, all the way down its sleek spine. As it disappears into the woods, I am left standing in awe, my hands outstretched and tingling.

I don't need anyone to help me find meaning. I call Marina—when she touches my head, neck, and spine, *I* feel tingling. Within months, the personal practice of Reiki becomes an essential component of my cult recovery. The gentle focus of *my own* hands, on my head, neck, and body supports me in the most surprising way: I literally feel my brain rewiring and nervous system settling—just as clearly as I'd heard the words, "It Is Over." I learn that hands can wake up, too.

"I want to go back to something you said earlier, if that's okay." Tammara, my therapist, has a specific tone in her voice when she is about to teach me something important.

"Of course," I say.

"When you were talking about how you are making progress in structuring your life around writing and running your business, you also said"—she glances at the notepad in her lap before continuing—"'I am not a disciplined person.' Do you remember that?"

"Sure do." *She has no idea just how undisciplined I really am!*

"Do you hear the self-judgment in that statement? What would it be like to reframe that into, 'I am creating more discipline in my life, especially around my writing'? Can you feel how different that is?"

I take a deep breath and recognize the difference, feeling it in my body. Tammara goes on to explain how this is not simply wordsmithing. There is a neurological difference in how an affirming statement is integrated by the brain, compared to a negative one. "Words matter."

So does having a good therapist—another essential component for my healing process. When I first walked into Tammara's office, one year post-Doug, I was unaware how programed my thinking still was. In CTL, every part of myself was identified as either pathology or process. Bad or good. Releasing deeply ingrained beliefs is not easy. It takes time and a lot of practice.

Tammara also guides me through the *internal conference*, where different parts of myself are invited to the table to discuss a particular issue. I am struggling with a decision to tell a friend I can no longer clean her house. Part of me loves maintaining this contact, another part feels guilty for letting her down, and another part feels harried and compulsive. Yet another part is clear that it's time to move on. With Tammara's help, all these inner voices are invited to the conference table. I am particularly distraught by my "harried self."

Tammara asks, "What are the advantages of your harried self? What help does it bring to the table?"

I am disoriented. Advantages? Nothing! My harried self is bad!

Quietly, she asks again. Circuitry in my brain ceases its familiar pattern—for just a moment. "I feel productive," tumbles out of my mouth, onto the table for everyone to see—and celebrate. Seeing the good in my harried self opens a door I'd locked tight during my eighteen years with Doug. Before this moment "harried" was hardwired as pathology and needed to be purged. Recognizing that the harried part of me had something positive, even productive to offer, is a game changer. Breaking out of dualistic "good and bad" thinking allows my nervous system—my entire being—to relax, welcoming nuance and the beauty of simply being human. I awaken to a new concept: *I don't have enemies within me.*

Controlling groups employ simplistic good-or-bad ideals dressed in fancy clothes, and expect members to strive for unattainable perfection. We become slaves to a goal that is noble or worthy but unrealistic. We defy what it is to be human while clambering for the right, the holy, the just.

❧

My nerdy teacher-self stirs and I begin to study. I dust off my discerning mind and get to work. Margaret Singer. Janja Lalich. Robert Jay Lifton. Steve Hassan. Reading the words of these cult recovery giants opens doors, flooding freedom into my mind, made narrow by Doug's doctrine. My days become filled with the twin heroes of compassion and understanding. I purchase more books in a two-year period than I had in the previous twenty, each book a companion for my adventure toward integration.

I talk as much as I read, making sense of the senseless. Writing is my therapy, too, as I'm free now to find words of my own. I rediscover creativity—no longer beleaguered by right and wrong—and am awed by this multi-faceted diamond.

> *I dream of Doug. His eyes are bright, but they do not have a hold on me anymore. I see he is a small man. I feel compassion for him.*

Free from the chains of his persuasive doctrine, I see Doug's humanness. He, who once was a giant, is now a small man. The truth is, after all is said and done, I don't wish him ill.

Funny, though—my father was small at the end of his life and I still feel love for him, even though he is dead. Not so, with Doug. In my everyday life, feelings toward him roam between regret, indifference, and sometimes pity. I find my dream a hopeful indication of greater generosity to come.

After six years of healing, who am I now? I am tougher and softer. More skeptical, without having lost my optimism. I laugh more. And I cry more. I am slower to judge, yet am much more discerning.

I love my life. Even on my worst days, of crushing insecurity or overwhelm, it takes but a few quiet breaths to remember who I am and the extraordinary bounty of my life.

I know a lot less than I did six years ago, because my world is so much bigger. I am a small fish, swimming and reflecting light, swallowing light, noticing the clouds—and the fallen stars—and how sometimes, light emerges from them, too.

Epilogue

DURING MY CTL DAYS, DOUG mandated that all members watch an eclectic mix of movies, including *The Matrix*, *The Blue Car*, and *Mother Teresa*. Every month or two, he'd assign a new one. I watched all these films with heightened awareness, striving to glean the significance he saw therein and apply it to my own life. My favorite was *Mother Teresa*, starring Olivia Hussey. I will never forget the class where Doug discussed this movie and its importance to him—there was an unusual softness in how he spoke—for he, too, revered Mother Teresa. He was inspired by her capacity to put her ego aside and not only listen to God's voice, but to *act* on His instructions.

My then-fragile psyche spiraled like a double helix: one strand my Catholic-girl naivety, the other, CTL indoctrination. At that time, I fervently believed Doug, too, would someday be revered for his contribution to society. Like Rudolph Steiner. Like Mother Teresa. I believed he would be that big. Bigger. He *was* that big in my psyche, which itself was made smaller through indoctrination. I clung to the hope of status by association—that when his teachings were finally recognized in the wider world, I, too, would be a somebody. Like one of Mother Teresa's devoted protégés, I would be Doug's.

Ugh.

Born a middle child in a big Irish-Italian Catholic family, my sense of self hovered small on the horizon—small, but ever hopeful, perhaps etched into my genes from my Irish Catholic ancestors. I stretch time and slip into the hungry body of a fair-haired, blue-eyed immigrant pushed from her emerald homeland, clinging to the thread of hope that pulled her across the wide Atlantic. My Italian Catholic relatives likely fled encroaching poverty, their eyes set on a new life—the push and pull of a refugee's destiny, pulsing them across the ocean.

New York harbor was a magnet for my weary, hopeful ancestors, arriving on these shores only to be greeted by cutting anti-Catholic bigotry. They were swiftly kicked to the bottom of this new society's pecking order. Shards of broken dreams were patched together as they survived and eventually created a life. A life beyond persecution and suffering. Fair hair and freckles mingled reluctantly with dark curls and olive skin, creating an unlikely blend that formed me and so many others.

Rapprochement. When I say the word in my head, my r's lull like the tide, as though I am fluent in French. If I had a ten-dollar bill for every time someone asked me "Are you French?" when they hear my name, I would've already completed the renovation of our home. But I'm not French, my home renovations stretch on for years, and I trip over my r's like the clumsy American speaker I am.

I learned about *rapprochement* in my post-CTL life, in Marina's kitchen. Not the political kind of rapprochement, although, of course, it is related. As we sipped from steaming mugs, we revisited territory explored together in my pre-CTL life: child development, including the work of Margaret Mahler and her astute observations of children fifteen to twenty-four months old, particularly their newfound mobility, crawling/walking/running, prompting a move away from the mother (or mother-figure) for exploration, and the return for reassurance.

Again and again, the child leaves: "You can't catch me!" But a loud sound, a new person, or hunger send the child scurrying back to Mother's safety. This back-and-forth—between the titillating unknown and the safety of maternal stability—is the ebb and flow of rapprochement. Without this developmental process, individuation— the transformative process that leads to an integrated, whole, and autonomous personality—is hindered and may be impossible.

Marina and I muse: *adults grow through rapprochement, too.* We run headlong into the wind, and when we run amuck or fly too close to the sun, we can return to the safety of "home," which is the growth we'd previously fully integrated. We are constantly building on the foundation of what we've completed. There is always more growing to do. There is great gentleness in this back-and-forth—no matter how long it takes or how many "mistakes" are made. The shuttle of life's loom passes again and again. It is never too late to find the anchor of our inner home. It is never too late to individuate.

I think authoritarianism is the travesty of someone claiming to know better than you what is best for you. It can be any doctrine— Catholicism, Marxism, Gaianism—*if we let it.* It can be any leader— Donald Trump, Hillary Clinton, your minister—*if we let them.* Any one of us can become an unethical, authoritarian leader—*if* we allow ourselves to become smitten with self-importance and follow the steps in the "cult leader's handbook" to gain a following. Any one of us can fall into or create an everyday cult.

After I got out, I discovered that people like being controlled as much as we like our freedom—it's woven into the finer structure of our brains. There is a time to conform, and a time to be autonomous. During a crisis, the masses rally as one for the greater good. We do this in times of natural disaster, in times of war. We offer meals and have each other's backs. This instinct, as natural as a hand rushing to cradle a bumped elbow, has taken a beating. But the thing about instinct is this: *it doesn't go away.*

Perhaps the group exodus of my former colleagues fleeing CTL was a version of healthy group instinct—an internal drive to get the hell out of an oppressive system. What one voice can't do, perhaps six can. I believe the #MeToo movement was fueled by a similar fire. Now, I wonder if we are ready to ignite the flames of honesty for another major step forward, for the betterment of humanity—to be honest about our personal experiences of abuses of power.

If enough of us are willing to come out of hiding, to speak in a unified voice, I have the feeling that our collective clarity could break through the forces that hinder, and may instead *support* human evolution. Stepping toward each other, defying false narratives that divide us, we become more human, more beautiful. As author and systems thinker Meg Wheatley asks, "Who do you choose to be?"[20] It's an option to isolate and stay quiet. It is also an option to step toward the future, into the unknown, until needing to return to the safety of the organized, integrated self. There is no pressure in the gentle back-and-forth of rapprochement, only growth.

In my mind, the potential for the betterment of humankind could very well lie in our capacity to grapple with destructive power dynamics and destigmatize mind control. When modern society is better able to recognize and understand this human vulnerability, positive change will naturally occur.

This change begins with nothing more and nothing less than individuals telling their own stories.

You have heard mine. Thank you for listening.

What is your story? I want to hear it.

Endnotes

1   Hassan, S. (2015). *Combating Cult Mind Control: The #1 Best-selling Guide to Protection, Rescue, and Recovery from Destructive Cults*. Freedom of Mind Press.

2   Summers, C. (2013). *What Goes Around: Two Books In One: Cracked Up to Be & Some Girls Are*. St. Martin's Griffin.

3   Bell, V. (2016, April 20). The Trippy State Between Wakefulness and Sleep. *The Atlantic*. https://www.theatlantic.com/science/archive/2016/04/deciphering-hypnagogia/478941

4   *Forget beach parties and all-night clubbing: Wealthy travelers are spending money differently, and it's created a massive $639 billion industry*. (2019, June 3). Business Insider. https://www.businessinsider.nl/wealthy-travelers-spending-habits-wellness-tourism-retreats-self-care-2019-6

5   Peck, S. M. (1998). *People of the Lie: The Hope for Healing Human Evil*. Touchstone.

6   Shulevitz, U. (1986). *The Treasure (Sunburst Book)* (First ed.). Square Fish.

7   Sams, J., Carson, D., & Werneke, A. C. (1999). *Medicine Cards: The Discovery of Power Through the Ways of Animals* (Revised ed.). St. Martin's Press.

8   Kramer, J., & Alstad, D. (1993). *The Guru Papers: Masks of Authoritarian Power*. Berkeley, Calif: Frog.

9   Norton, C. E., & Alighieri, D. (2012). *The Divine Comedy*; Ulan Press.

10 Shanola Hampton (born May 27, 1977) is an American actress

best known for her role as Veronica Fisher on Showtime dramedy Shameless.

11 Carey, B. (2007, November 19). *Denial - Psychology - Mental Health and Behavior.* The New York Times. https://www.nytimes. com/2007/11/20/health/research/20deni.html

12 *Holy Bible: King James Version*

13 Lifton, R. J. (2019). Losing Reality: *On Cults, Cultism, and the Mindset of Political and Religious Zealotry.* The New Press.

14 *snap.* (n.d.). The Merriam-Webster.Com Dictionary. Retrieved February 22, 2021, from https://www.merriam-webster.com/ dictionary/snap

15 *shock.* (n.d.). The Merriam-Webster.Com Dictionary. Retrieved February 22, 2021, from https://www.merriam-webster.com/ dictionary/shock

16 Al-Din Rumi, J., Barks, C., & Moyne, J. (2004). *The Essential Rumi, New Expanded Edition* (Reprint ed.). HarperOne.

17 Kimmerer, R. W. (2015). *Braiding Sweetgrass: Indigenous Wisdom, Scientific Knowledge and the Teachings of Plants* (First Paperback ed.). Milkweed Editions.

18 *Theodore Roethke Quotes.* (n.d.). BrainyQuote. Retrieved February 22, 2021, from https://www.brainyquote.com/quotes/theodore_ roethke_137366

19 Siegel, D. J. (2010). *Mindsight: The New Science of Personal Transformation* (Illustrated ed.). Bantam.

20 Wheatley, M. J. (2017). *Who Do We Choose To Be?: Facing Reality, Claiming Leadership, Restoring Sanity* (1st ed.). Berrett-Koehler Publishers.

Acknowledgments

A FRIEND ASKED ME WHAT was most surprising about writing a book. In the past, my impression of an author—any author—was a lone person, scribing stories on an island. Today, I know it takes a village to write a book.

My village began with Paula Diaco, my book coach and now dear friend who cheered and guided me beyond the point of no return. With Paula, came a team of gifted writers: Pat Goudey O'Brien (whose ability to grasp the intent trapped in my jumbled sentences came in handy when she became my trusted editor); Mary Hill (whose artistry adorns this book cover); Markey Read; and C. Jane Taylor—all of whom managed to share something positive about my writing every week that I showed up. It took me a long time to believe them. Their affirmations, combined with how much I learned through their mastery, gave me courage when doubt doubled down on me. Courtney Jenkins stepped in at the tail end, with her editing wizardry focused on form and flow. Thank you, dear Courtney.

Before this, came the many who helped me heal to the point that I could speak about my cultic experience without shaking uncontrollably—a deep and dear circle of friends, family and professionals: Lisa Dimondstein (whose photography and advice is as invaluable as our countless walks in the woods), Jan Oliver, Margot Prendergast, Sarah Forbes (whose professionalism, keen eye, and calm offered me anchor when I needed it), Barbara Benton, and Heather Watrous. I can't write these six names without including me, Gerette—together we *are* the Seven Sisters who welcomed me back after I had strayed. Mark Laxer and Marcie Vallette, my allies whose insight and levity are a rare and essential combination. Theresa Matocha, LICSW, my integrative therapist of four years (without whom, I might still be shaking), and Jane Kast, MA Psychologist, with whom the words "as needed" affirms for me the natural cycle of a healthy therapist/client relationship. Caro Thompson, whose clarity and compassion taught me how to speak of indigenous cultures without degrading them or myself. Jayne Allister, whose unconditional acceptance provided me haven when I most needed it. Special thanks to Muriel Zimmer, who championed me in my early days and to Marie Turmel, who was first to read my manuscript knowing nothing of my story. Their thoughtful recommendations are woven into the book.

I will forever be grateful to the members of the Stowe Area Toastmasters group where I learned to speak; Vermont Studio Center in Johnson, Vermont; and for Flavia Cosma of the International Writers' and Artists' Residency, in Val David, Quebec, where I could first utter the words, "I am a writer."

There can be a point in the cult recovery process where one's identity shifts from cult survivor to *thriver*. Seems to me, this is largely supported by the company we keep day after day, week after week. Now in our 'year after year,' my Tuesday morning writing partnership with Edie Yovu and Nancy Mosher has unquestionably ushered me into this transformation and also boosted my self-knowledge IQ. My new team, sparked by the I Got Out initiative, has further contributed to my capacity to thrive in my post-cult life. Special thanks to cult expert Steven Hassan, PhD, whose enthusiasm for #iGotOut affirms the goodness of his heart, and Sarah Edmondson, who graciously read every word of this book, bringing me to tears with her words in the foreword. My new best friends are Lisa and Casey, who rock my world with their unparalleled ardor, skill diversity, sound advice, and light-hearted partnership in what matters most, second only to my family. Frederic, Sonya, Marquis, and Luke: your steadfastness, honesty, and encouragement fuels the ship I am steering through bringing this book into the world. My cup runneth over with love and gratitude.

About the Author

GERETTE BUGLION WAS BORN ON Long Island, New York, where she was tossed around by waves at Jones Beach as a young child. Her northward migration started at five years of age, when her large family moved to Dutchess County, New York, to farm. Cows, sheep, and an untold number of cats accompanied the rest of her childhood, until she fledged to the northern woods. Her work and passions merged in caring for others as an elementary school teacher, special educator, house parent for people with special needs, and as a hiking guide. Her greatest accomplishments include parenting two exceptional young adults, marrying an extraordinarily understanding man, and escaping from what she calls "an everyday cult." Her current work as a cult awareness consultant arises from her dedication to helping others navigate and avoid controlling power dynamics in destructive cultic groups. She is a founding collaborator for the #iGotOut movement (www.igotout.org), which encourages all who have been impacted by mind control and cultic involvement to tell their stories. Learn more at Gerette's website, gerettebuglion.com.

Also Available from Rootstock Publishing:

The Atomic Bomb on My Back
Taniguchi Sumiteru

Blue Desert
Celia Jeffries

*China in Another
Time: A Personal Story*
Claire Malcolm Lintilhac

*Fly with A Murder of Crows:
A Memoir*
Tuvia Feldman

The Inland Sea: A Mystery
Sam Clark

Junkyard at No Town
J.C. Myers

*The Language of Liberty:
A Citizen's Vocabulary*
Edwin C. Hagenstein

A Lawyer's Life to Live
Kimberly B. Cheney

Lifting Stones
Doug Stanfield

The Lost Grip: Poems
Eva Zimet

Lucy Dancer
Story and Illustrations by Eva Zimet

Nobody Hitchhikes Anymore
Ed Griffin-Nolan

*Preaching Happiness:
Creating a Just and Joyful World*
Ginny Sassaman

*Red Scare in the Green Mountains:
Vermont in the McCarthy Era
1946–1960*
Rick Winston

Safe as Lightning: Poems
Scudder H. Parker

Street of Storytellers
Doug Wilhelm

*Tales of Bialystok:
A Jewish Journey from
Czarist Russia to America*
Charles Zachariah Goldberg

*To the Man in the Red Suit:
Poems*
Christina Fulton

*Uncivil Liberties:
A Novel*
Bernie Lambek

The Violin Family
Melissa Perley;
Illustrated by Fiona Lee Maclean

Walking Home
Celia Ryker

Wave of the Day: Collected Poems
Mary Elizabeth Winn

*Whole Worlds Could Pass Away:
Collected Stories*
Rickey Gard Diamond

*You Have a Hammer:
Building Grant Proposals for
Social Justice*
Barbara Floersch